AGAINST THE CLOCK

A Story of Faith, Fatherhood, Basketball, and the Relentless Pursuit of Purpose

by

DAMIEN ARGRETT

ISBN: 979-8-218-89487-0
Printed in the United States of America
For permissions or speaking engagements, contact:
damien@bobwbasketball.com

Dedication

To my mother, Joanne, who shaped my life from the beginning.

To my father, Morris Holmes, your passing turned me into an animal, but your memory still guides me every day.

To my wife, Bria, and my son, Kaison, you are my peace, my joy, and my purpose.

Acknowledgments

I want to thank the people who poured into me, believed in me, and stood with me through every chapter of my life.

To my mother, Joanne, you saw something in me long before basketball ever did.

To my father, Morris Holmes, your passing lit a fire in me that never went out.

To my sister Tanya, thank you for always standing by me.

To John Davis, for caring about me as a player, and even more, as a man.

To Dave Davis, thank you for guiding me at moments when I didn't know I needed it.

To Kim Davis, thank you for loving me like your own son.

To Mrs. Gore, may you rest in peace. Thank you for believing in me before I believed in myself.

To Bria, you walked into my life exactly when God wanted you to. Thank you for loving me, challenging me, and helping me build a life I'm proud of.

To my son, Kaison, you changed everything. You gave my life new purpose and a new heartbeat.

To every player, coach, parent, and supporter of BOBW, you are part of this story, too.

Table of Contents

Prologue

This book is called Against the Clock. Not because I was running out of time, but because from the very beginning, I always felt like I had to play catch-up. I wasn't the kid who grew up in camps with trainers or AAU programs pushing me forward. I wasn't the star with a guaranteed path. I was just a boy from the South Bronx trying to figure it out, step by step.

When I think about what Against the Clock means, I think about moments that press on your chest and make you decide who you really are.

I think about my freshman year at South when I walked off the bench and quit the team. I can still picture Coach Parker standing over a pile of varsity laundry, looking up just long enough to say, "You'll never play for South Rowan again." That one sentence lived in my head for years. I carried it around like a weight in my pocket, heavier every time I thought about it.

But life has a way of shifting when you keep going. I grew ten inches, found a work ethic I didn't even know I had, and by my junior year, the same man who once told me I'd never set foot on his gym floor again was inviting me back to workouts. To this day, I don't think he remembers saying it, or even remembers me from back then. I was just a skinny freshman, easy to overlook. And when I walked into his P.E. class as a junior, ten inches taller and a completely different kid, he probably didn't recognize the same boy who once stood in front of him saying he didn't care if he ever played for South Rowan.

I think about the summer before that season. I'd just come off a great run at team camp, ready for the year I'd been waiting for, and then the news no one is ready for: my mom and sister took my father to the hospital and came home with the news that he was gone. The house went silent in a way words can't describe. I went to the gym, turned off the lights, and shot in the dark because I didn't know what else to do. Every ball that dropped through the net felt like a prayer: make him proud.

Then there was the night everything clicked, forty points and twenty-two rebounds, breaking the single game records in both for the Raiders vs Northwest Cabarrus High School. The game slowed down so much that night that I could feel it in my hands. The next day, Mike London from the Salisbury Post showed up with a box of Blow Pops and a notepad. For the first time, I felt seen. Really seen. And from that moment forward, I chased the work, not the eyes on me. I fell in love with the feeling of effort turning into results, and I understood something important: the lights always find the people who keep working.

In college, there was Barton. We were getting beat bad. I'd been lifting, watching film, living in the gym, and when my number finally came, I gave them eighteen points and nine boards in limited minutes. That night tilted my career. I wasn't a role player pretending anymore; I belonged.

Years later, across an ocean, I felt the clock again in Romania. First game back from a groin injury, and I knew if I didn't show out, I was going home. I went for twenty-five and thirteen against the best team in the country at the time: Cluj Napoca. That night saved my job and, maybe, my professional career. And much later, after planes, passports, and empty apartments, I felt it again, but this time at home.

When Benchwarmers Sports Complex shut down, I lost my gym overnight. I wasn't broke, but I was unsure where my business would go. My high school coach, John Davis, helped me hold it together until I could secure a partnership with the Town of Mooresville. That moment didn't start BOBW Basketball; it kept it alive. It rooted it in the Mooresville and Lake Norman area, where it could keep impacting kids and changing lives. Those are the beats of Against the Clock. Not panic, but purpose. Not fear, but faith under pressure.

If you read this book, you will understand that life will throw adversity your way, but it won't last. Most of the time, you're being tested by God to see if you really want what you say you want, or to see if you're ready for the blessing you asked for. You can't control what happens, but you can always control your response. Keep showing up. Keep working. Keep believing.

Now I'm a husband, a father, and the founder of BOBW Basketball Services—one of the biggest programs in the area and one that's impacted thousands of kids. My story is proof that even when the odds are against you, if you keep showing up, keep working, and keep believing, you can build a life and a legacy worth remembering.

This is my story.

This is Against the Clock.

CHAPTER 1

BRONX BEGINNINGS

Mitchell Projects stood twenty stories high, a concrete giant in the middle of the South Bronx that never slept. Sirens, laughter, car horns, somebody arguing out a window, gunshots, and music blasting from somewhere in the distance were all part of the rhythm. By the time I was old enough to understand anything about life, I had already learned that the Bronx had its own heartbeat. Loud, wild, unpredictable, but familiar.

We lived on the seventeenth floor; high enough to see the neighborhood stretching out like a maze of brick, steam, and constant movement. From our apartment window, we could see other boroughs in the distance, with Manhattan sitting right across from us, maybe a fifteen-minute walk away. Most days, though, we stayed right in our projects, trying to live life and make it through the day like everyone else.

People hear "South Bronx" and picture danger around every corner but growing up in it felt different. It wasn't all chaos and fear. It was home. Most families were just trying to get by, work hard, mind their business, and keep their kids safe. Yes, we saw crime. Yes, violence existed. Drugs were everywhere, with crack vials scattered near the trash cans and people nodding off on benches. Heroin needles showed up on the courts and near the playgrounds so often that you had to watch where you stepped, where you sat, and where you put your hands so you didn't accidentally get poked.

But even with all of that, I never felt like we were in danger or that we were poor. My mother worked her ass off to make sure we never felt that way. She had this "go-get-it" mentality that never shut off. Every single day, she left our apartment with purpose, carrying the weight of responsibility without ever letting it show. She was the real engine of our family, and her work ethic has stayed with me to this day.

I have a lot of memories from those years, but one that stands out most is my sixth-grade graduation from P.S. 154. Both my mom and dad were so proud. I received a bunch of academic awards, and my mom celebrated me like it was the biggest moment in the world. She gave me money and gifts, and took me out to eat that night. Those are the moments that stick with you, the ones where you feel seen and valued.

I also remember the trips to the Bronx Zoo with my sister, Button, and her kids—the times she took us to the carnival, and all the little things in between. My mom hardly ever said no. If she had it to give, it was ours. And even on the days she didn't have it, she still found a way.

The Bronx had a smell you could never forget. A mix of city exhaust, corner-store food, hot pavement in the summertime, hallway bleach, and whatever the projects had cooking that day. Sometimes, it smelled like fried chicken from the apartment next door. Sometimes, it smelled like yesterday's trash left out too long. Sometimes, it was just straight-up New York: loud and unapologetic. But when you stepped into 17F, the whole atmosphere shifted. The scent of Pine-Sol mixed with whatever was cooking; it always felt like safety.

My mother managed apartments on 161st Street, not far from Aunt Cheryl's projects. She loved that job and took pride in the way she handled everything: managing tenants, fixing problems, and keeping order. My sister, Tanya and my brother, Brandon, and I would go to work with her sometimes if we had a half day or were sick. We'd also hit the barbershop near her job—a usual stop for us.

Right across the street from her building was a Florida Fried Chicken spot we went to all the time. We'd grab a box of chicken and fries, a slice of pizza, a whole pie, or Jamaican beef patties, which were my favorite. She'd give us markers and paper to keep us busy, and I'd spend the time drawing cartoon characters, superheroes, and anything my mind could put together.

Her office had a small playground right outside, and we'd run around and play for hours, waiting for her shift to end. My mother was always strict but fair with the tenants, and many of them liked her because of her calm demeanor and the way she stayed professional, no matter the situation. She always did what she said she would do and never lied to anyone. One of her tenants used to braid her hair for her, and I had the biggest crush on her back then. She would refer to me as her boyfriend, and I'm not even sure I knew what that meant at the time, but I knew I liked her a lot.

Inside our apartment, my mother kept order. We all had chores: cleaning our rooms and keeping things neat. I was always responsible for taking out the trash. Every night, there was a hot meal on the stove: fried chicken, pork chops, spaghetti, meatloaf, salmon patties. And on the days she did not feel like cooking, she would bring home Chinese food, pizza, or chicken from Florida Fried Chicken. Part of our routine was making sure to take the meat out early so it could defrost before she got home. If we forgot, the whole evening got thrown off, and she let us know it.

My dad, Morris cooked sometimes too, but I never really liked his meals. One dish in particular, lima beans and neckbones, was something I dreaded. He helped with money when he could, but he never had a stable job. He always had a little hustle or some odd job to bring something into the home, but most of the weight fell on my mother. There were times she resented him for that. We could see the frustration on her face, and it made us upset, too. But she never allowed us to disrespect him, and he never allowed it either. When we were young, all he had to do was give us a certain look, and we straightened up immediately.

My dad was not someone who showed much emotion. I remember those poker games when I was in high school, and if he had a few drinks, he would laugh and cut up a little. But outside of that, I have no real memories of him crying or showing much emotion at all, aside from anger at times. I cannot remember him saying, "I love you." Maybe that is why I tell my son, Kaison every chance I get. And honestly, it is probably why I struggle with showing emotion myself. Almost every man I grew up around, my uncles included, kept everything bottled up. Back then, expressing yourself felt like weakness.

When we had to take clothes to the laundromat, we had a whole system. Certain dryers were better than others, so we rushed to get the good ones. While our clothes dried, we watched them closely. People could take your stuff out just to put theirs in, and some would steal clothes if they saw something they liked. If we had leftover quarters, we would hit the corner store for chips or candy.

The elevators in the projects were a gamble. When the lights flickered and the metal groaned, you never knew if they would take you up or

4

break down halfway. It was never a surprise to step inside and find someone had peed in the corner or that trash was scattered across the floor. And every now and then, the whole elevator would get stuck. Sitting in that metal box felt like forever, until the fire department finally came to get you out. When the elevators were out completely, we took the stairs. Walking seventeen flights was one thing, but doing it with bags of laundry or groceries was a different story. That was a workout for sure.

One side of the stairwell was basically home to a homeless man who lived there. You could smell him before the door even opened—heavy, sour, strong enough to make your eyes water. At night, when I had to take the trash to the incinerator, I would sprint, holding my breath, praying he would not jump out. I did not understand then that he was just a man going through hard times. When you are a kid, shadows feel alive.

There were funny and memorable characters in our neighborhood, too. All of us—me, Ramon, Kareem, and the rest—went to P.S. 154. Ramon and Kareem were my closest friends from school. We played basketball in the park during recess and two-hand touch football in the winter. Those were the days. The games were always fun and competitive, and we were inseparable from the earliest years all the way up to seventh grade, when we each went to different junior high schools. Even though they lived up the block, we hung out almost every day.

We also played *skelzies*, one of our favorite games. At lunchtime in sixth grade, we would walk to the store to buy something to eat, or to pick up clay for our tops. Most of the time, we grabbed a slice, or four chicken wings with fries, or pork fried rice. That always hit the spot, and you could usually get it for about four dollars. After we ate, we would be right back on the sidewalk, sliding our bottle caps across the chalked-up board, arguing over calls, celebrating big shots like they were championship plays. We played that game for hours.

There was Natasha, who was mature for her age and always had on the latest sneakers and gear. Her mother did not play around. She was tough on her, strict, and one of those parents you respected even if you did not understand why at the time. Vera was another girl who was cool. She was smart, quick-witted, and could talk junk with the best of them. Gordon was a quiet kid whose family was deep into religion. He did not say much, but he was probably one of the fastest kids at P.S. 154.

Marisol, a girl from the twentieth floor, was one of my first crushes. A Spanish girl with a sweet family. We dated for a few days in sixth grade, or at least that is what we called it. Looking back, I do not even know if she liked me. But that was New York. You grew up fast without even realizing it. By the time I got to fifth and sixth grade, everybody was dating each other, and doing things kids had no business doing. The city pushed you forward quicker than you were ready for. Unless your parents kept you in the house, you were going to see or experience things you had no business being around at that age.

Tanya looked out for me in ways I didn't fully understand until I got older. She protected me, made sure no one messed with me, and, honestly, was better at basketball than I was, early on. When the older kids picked teams, she got chosen before I did. But whenever she could, she would tell the boys to pick her brother. She even let me wear her shoes sometimes since our sizes were close and we were both into fashion and sneakers.

When we moved down to North Carolina, Tanya was a senior at South Rowan High School. She had planned on playing basketball, but her transcripts didn't come in on time, so she never got the chance. She finished the year and then started working different odd jobs. I remember one of her jobs was at Hardee's, and she would bring home chicken and whatever food she could for us to eat.

Tanya also drove us around whenever my dad was not available, because my mother did not drive. She never liked how narrow the streets were, so Tanya became the one who drove us everywhere. As I got older and got back into basketball, she was the one taking me to and from workouts and practices too. Sometimes, she did it reluctantly, but somehow, I usually got where I needed to be.

Brandon and I shared a room back then. I used to get mad when he touched my things, but that was just normal brother stuff. I would talk him into giving me his leftover food or money, and most of the time, he would give in.

My uncles were another story. My Uncle Melvin once stole my favorite bike right off me on my birthday—the one with the trick sticks. We had run into him on 3rd Avenue. He looked at the bike, looked at me, pushed me off, and rode away. I remember yelling for him to come back, and taking off running after him, but he disappeared within seconds. That was Melvin—wild, unpredictable, and living life on his own terms. He's still in New York today, but he's changed a lot. He keeps a steady job now and does what he needs to do.

Uncle Duane had his moments, too. One time, he came over asking for a glass of water. While we were in the back with my mom, he unplugged the VCR and vanished. The faucet was still running when we came out. That was Duane. But he wasn't all bad. He painted our apartment, helped my mom with odd jobs, and always tried to be useful in his own way. When we moved to North Carolina, he later followed and became a regular at our kitchen table during poker nights—smoking, laughing loudly, and filling the whole house with a kind of energy that felt familiar. He eventually got married down here. They divorced a few years back, and he now lives on his own, just moving through life the best way he knows how.

Not all our adventures were harmless. One day, my sister and I were flying paper airplanes out the window. I was around seven, she was twelve, and for some reason, we decided it would be a great idea to set one on fire. We watched it float and drift like it was the coolest thing ever, until it glided straight into a neighbor's apartment and lit her curtains. Seconds later, she came storming upstairs, yelling in Spanish, and my mother handled the situation with a braided extension cord. My dad rarely whipped us, but my mom made sure you remembered the lesson.

And then there was the Ninja Turtle incident. Tanya, our cousins, Joe, James, and I were walking down 3rd Avenue when we saw a guy dressed as one of the turtles. I still don't know if I was dared or if I just lost my mind for a second, but I walked right up to him, ran back a few steps, and punched him in the face. I thought it was hilarious, until he started chasing me. He chased me for five blocks, and I ran like my life depended on it. I did not go back to 3rd Avenue for weeks after that. We did crazy stuff like that all the time growing up. It was normal to us. Just another day in the Bronx.

Holidays in the Bronx meant going to my grandmother, Alice's, house. She had the kind of home every grandma seemed to have back then: plastic-covered furniture, spotless floors, and bowls of those hard red candies no one ever bought but every older Black woman somehow had. She always gave us a little something around our birthdays and at Christmas, and even the smallest gift felt big coming from her.

In the summers, we went to Crotona Park for picnics. Aunt Cheryl would bring her fried chicken or Spanish rice and beans. We brought burgers, hot dogs, buns, and shish kebabs, and my grandmother usually showed up with potato salad, egg salad, chips, and drinks. Somehow, our uncles always found a way to come through, grab a plate, hang around just long enough to joke with everyone, and then slip out. They didn't just steal from us; they stole from Aunt Cheryl too. But when they came back around, none of us kids ever said anything. It was like it never happened. I'm sure the adults talked about it among themselves, but for us, it was just part of the rhythm of those family gatherings.

We didn't see my grandmother often back then, but when she moved South later, we grew closer. She loved seeing my basketball articles in the newspaper whenever she could get her hands on them. She passed away during my junior year of college, but the pride she had in me still sticks with me today.

Mom had a gift for making life feel special even when money was tight. Trips to Coney Island or Orchard Beach, ice skating at Rockefeller Center, new clothes at Christmas; she always made it happen. One year, we got the Super Nintendo and a few bills in envelopes. Another year, after losing her job managing those apartments, she still found a way to give my sister and me two hundred dollars each. It wasn't much, but it felt like a fortune.

Joe and James, and their sisters, Shaunice and Vernell, were like siblings to us. Joe and James protected us, looked out for us, and as I got older, they passed down their old clothes and sneakers, which always felt like a blessing. James was athletic. He was strong, fast, fearless, flipping off anything like it was nothing. Joe wasn't into sports, but he stayed clean and fresh with his sneakers and tapes, and he had a smooth way about him that everyone respected.

Shaunice and Vernell were the ones who hooked me up with girls. They always knew who liked who and who thought I was cute, and

9

they weren't shy about letting me know. They kept me in the loop long before I had any idea what to do with the information.

We spent a lot of time together. Whenever Aunt Cheryl or Uncle Dave gave us a couple dollars, we would walk to the corner store and load up on Now and Laters and Wise chips, grabbing whatever looked good. Those little trips felt like big adventures. And whenever someone bothered us, we never faced it alone. When a kid named Horace started bullying us, Joe, James, and our cousin David handled it in minutes. Whatever they said or did worked, because Horace never bothered us again.

Aunt Linda was my mother's other sister who lived in the Bronx, but we hardly saw her or spoke to her. Even when we did, she barely talked to us, and always carried a mean, standoffish way about her. My mother and Aunt Linda never had the best relationship, but Aunt Linda and Aunt Cheryl were close, so we would see her from time to time at cookouts or family gatherings. We were all on the same side of the family, but it didn't always feel that way.

David and Bobby were her sons. David was cool, quiet, and talked fast, moving at his own pace, but still easy enough to be around. Bobby was more of a loner. He kept to himself, barely interacted with us when we were younger, and never really joined in with the rest of the cousins. By the time he started opening up as we all got older, the rest of us already had years of memories, jokes, games, and moments he had never been a part of. David too, in a way. They were family, but they were never really part of that tight circle we grew up in.

On my dad's side of the family, things were different. He had children outside of my mother: Boo, Kevin, Barbra, Deserie, and Button. Boo and I became close before he was shot and killed in the Bronx, which stayed with me for a long time. Kevin was known for loving Michael Jackson and Jordans, always dancing or showing off whatever sneakers he had on. My older sisters had kids around my age, so cousins were everywhere on that side of the family too.

My dad, Morris Holmes whom everyone called "Easy," wasn't always around consistently. One of my earliest memories is taking the train upstate in the cold to visit him in prison when I was five or six. And even when he was home, life with him came in waves. My mother stood by him through a lot, loving him in a way only she could understand, even as everything around us kept shifting.

Easy was the family enforcer, the one you called when something went wrong and needed to be handled. He was an imposing figure at 6'2", solid build, dark skin, braids, and a presence that walked into a room before he did. He had a kind heart, no question, but if you didn't know him, you'd definitely fear him. And even if you *did* know him, you still didn't want to cross him.

We went to more funerals than most kids—uncles, aunts, grandparents, and then my brother, Boo. He was shot and killed in the Bronx near McCombs Road, where his mother lived. That one hit hard. We had only recently gotten to know him, but blood is blood, and he was everything we wanted in a big brother. He would stay with us for a few days at a time, and it always made me proud to tell my friends when he was around.

Boo had cornrows, just like my father. That was a thing on my dad's side of the family; most of the boys grew their hair out, kept it braided, and kept it long. I tried it briefly a couple of times, but it never felt like me. I always preferred a short cut, a *Caesar,* as they call it in New York, or a simple fade.

Death became something we understood early, which is strange to say, but that was life in the Bronx. It was around us, part of the background, and something you learned to process long before you should have had to.

Outside, the soundtrack was classic New York. You might hear Nice & Smooth, Biggie, LL Cool J blasting from windows, and every now and then, some Shabba Ranks, Wu-Tang Clan, or the Fugees shaking the block. Kids yelling on the street. Buses screeching. People arguing, laughing, living loud right outside our building. The bodega across the street had everything: chips, candy, hero sandwiches, cigarettes... That store was part of our routine. Every couple of days, my sister or I would be sent to grab cigarettes for my parents. My mother smoked Newports; my father smoked Kools. Looking back, it's wild how easily we could buy that stuff at such a young age, but the bodega workers knew all the neighborhood kids and who our parents were. That would never fly today, especially in North Carolina. You need an ID for everything now.

My dad's car embarrassed us. When we pulled into the projects, we'd duck down like we were hiding from the world. Funny thing is, most people in the Bronx didn't even have cars. Kids grew up fast there. By ten or eleven, you were already thinking about girls, or at least trying to. I had a skinny frame, a gap in my teeth, and a head I still needed to grow into, but my mother kept us clean. So, even when I didn't look like much, I always walked with confidence.

One of my favorite memories was when Rod Strickland came through the projects. He signed one of my basketball cards. I used to skip lunch just to buy packs. That autograph made me believe I could become something. I collected cards for years, but during the move down South, I lost a ton of them. To this day, I can only imagine what they'd be worth. After Kaison was born, I started collecting again. I never opened the packs; I figured one day, he'll get the fun of tearing them open himself.

We made our own fun in the Bronx. We rode bikes up and down the block, flipped on old mattresses, and shot on milk crates or wire hangers twisted into hoops inside apartments. One year, my mother even bought us rollerblades, and we rode them all through the hood like we owned every hallway and sidewalk. When you don't have much, imagination fills in the gaps. Some of my best memories came from nothing.

Growing up, basketball was everything to me. I used to dream about playing in the NBA, not because of money or fame, but because I genuinely loved the game. Watching Michael Jordan in the 90s felt like watching a real-life superhero. In the inner city, you were either a Knicks fan or a Bulls fan, and most kids I knew were riding with Jordan. His athleticism, his skill, the way he moved—every kid wanted to be like Mike.

I would sit glued to the television on nights when the Bulls played, studying every move. I remember one game against the Magic where he hit this wild fadeaway jumper. I couldn't believe it. As soon as the play ended, I ran downstairs to the court, determined to try it myself. I mimicked the move perfectly, but what I didn't realize was that landing on concrete hits a whole lot differently than hardwood. My tailbone was hurting for weeks, but that moment stayed with me. That was the first time I understood what it meant to feel the game; to chase something so much bigger than where you were.

Years later, in high school, the game slowed down for me in a way I had never felt before. The night I scored 40 points and grabbed 22 rebounds, I knew something special had happened. It was surreal. The next morning, I had to take the SAT, and after finishing, John picked me up with several copies of the Salisbury Post in the car. I was on the front page of the sports section: "Argrett Scores 40 Points, Grabs 22 Rebounds." Breaking two single-game scoring records and rising from nowhere to become one of the best players in the area; stories like mine didn't happen often. Most players followed the traditional path: travel ball, middle school, JV, varsity. I came a completely different route, and that night was the first time I truly believed I belonged. I wouldn't have that feeling again until my sophomore year of college. Once it returned, though, it stayed. When the game slows down for you like that, there's no better feeling in the world.

The night before we moved, someone got shot right next to our van. My dad yelled for us to duck. In a weird way, it felt like the city itself was telling us it was time to go. We took the Amtrak south. I still remember the hot chocolate on the train and spotting my grandfather waiting for us at the station in Mooresville. He drove us back to his place: an old trailer surrounded by quiet and open space. To us, it looked like luxury. It was bigger than our apartment, it had room to move, and the silence felt like breathing for the first time.

My grandfather had an old Carolina blue truck with no air conditioning. Riding in it during the summer felt like sitting inside a hair dryer. But he also had a Cadillac he took us out in sometimes. The Cadillac had real AC, and that car felt like heaven. We had chores at his place too. He had two dogs we were responsible for feeding and cleaning up after, and we helped him mow the yard. My mom cooked meals and paid for groceries to help out however she could. It wasn't easy, but we made it work because she stayed determined.

The kid next door, Matt, had a hoop and a trampoline he let me use. We were tight for a while. He had stacks of VHS tapes and would let me borrow whatever I wanted. I remember he had White Men Can't Jump, and I watched it like it was gospel. His family didn't mind us borrowing movies, as long as we brought them back. My mom was always nervous about borrowing things from other people, but we did it anyway. Later, when we moved to West 22nd, Matt and I still attended the same middle school, but we barely talked. That's how childhood friendships go: close one season, distant the next.

14

Leaving New York hit me in a way I didn't expect. Before we left, we stopped by Aunt Cheryl's to say goodbye. I had grown up around her kids, and spent so many days in and out of her place that walking away felt like closing the door on a whole chapter of my childhood. It felt like we were leaving a piece of ourselves behind. But that move ended up changing everything for the better.

North Carolina was slower, quieter, and different. Once it hit me that we weren't going back, I realized how big the change really was. We came down with barely anything; no money, and no real plan beyond staying with my grandfather. But that move shaped everything I would eventually become.

The South Bronx raised me in ways a basketball court never could. It taught me toughness and how to hold my ground. It taught me to hustle for everything, to never expect anything to be handed to me, and to never fold under pressure. Where I grew up, excuses didn't matter. If you wanted something, you worked for it. If you wanted respect, you earned it.

I learned early that you didn't need to be the loudest in the room; your actions spoke louder than anything you could say. That mindset followed me long after I left the Bronx. It shaped how I moved, how I competed, and later, how I coached and led others. It was loud, gritty, unforgiving, and it built me. The Bronx was wild, dangerous, creative, loving, and unforgettable, but it was home. And everything that came after started right there.

CHAPTER 2

MIDDLE SCHOOL: ADJUSTING TO THE SOUTH

Corriher-Lipe Middle School felt like stepping into a world running at half-speed. Everything about it—the air, the voices, the space between buildings—felt slower than what my body was used to. Coming from the Bronx, where you wake up to noise, energy, motion, and people everywhere, North Carolina felt open, quiet, and strangely calm.

My first day walking into that school still plays in my mind. I had on a flat top, a thick New York accent I didn't even know I had, and a pair of black K-Swiss shoes that belonged to my sister. They were clean though, and they became my basketball shoes. The moment I stepped into my first class, every head turned. It wasn't rude; just curious. I stuck out instantly. After class, kids came up to me asking, "What's your name?" "Where you from?" "You talk funny." They meant it harmlessly. They weren't used to New York kids, just like I wasn't used to being somewhere everyone said "yes ma'am" and "no sir." In the Bronx, you barely say hello unless you know somebody.

I never liked eating school lunch, not even in New York, so I brought sandwiches and chips from home. The only thing I'd buy were the cookies; they were always good. PE was one of my favorite periods. It gave me a comfortable space to show who I was. Running, jumping, throwing, catching—those things came naturally. And in middle school, if you could do that, you were automatically someone people gravitated toward. Being from New York, I naturally thought I was the best at everything anyway, and that the South was slow. Crazy that perception you have as a kid of places and people you don't know anything about. P.E was always my favorite class since I can remember. Even in New York, we would run relay races around the gym, and the fastest person always got love from everyone in the class. I was usually top 5 or so in racing, depending on the day.

I met Ashley, Tasha, Raheisa, and Lateria early on. They were friendly, funny, and made me feel like I wasn't as out of place as I thought. The first boy who approached me was Steven Venable. He didn't come over smiling; he came over sizing me up, making sure I wasn't soft. That's just how middle school boys are. But once he realized I was cool and that I could hoop, he was sold. We clicked instantly and stayed tight through middle school and high school.

People waved at you for no reason. Kids spoke politely. Teachers were calm. Even the way people walked seemed slower. The South had its own rhythm, and slowly but surely, I adjusted. As far as me fitting in and finding my way, Basketball helped more than anything. Coach Ron Riddle was my history teacher and the basketball coach. When I told him I could play, his eyes lit up. That was always the theme of my life: if I could play, I could belong. I made the team both years, and led the school in scoring. Corriher-Lipe wasn't known for sports. We didn't win a single game in the two years I played there. Our closest matchups were always against China Grove, but even they found ways to beat us. Still, I was the best player on that team, and it gave me a confidence I hadn't felt before. It made me walk around school like I was untouchable, which also made me a class clown. I talked back, joked too much, and pushed boundaries.

Steven was the same way. We would pick on kids, laugh too loud, and do stupid middle school stuff for no reason other than trying to be cool. Some afternoons, we would go over to Casey's house which was down the road. The town of Landis where Corriher-Lipe isn't big at all, so some students would walk to and from school. There were a couple gas stations and basketball courts we would frequent on nice days to shoot hoops or get a snack after school. Also, the Landis pool was right across the street from the school. My siblings and I would go there a few times each summer to swim. Those were some awesome days. That pool would be packed and still is to this day when I drive by there on a hot summer day.

My first organized basketball game ever was in seventh grade. Before that, the only other time I even tried out for a team was at my old elementary school P.S. 154 in the Bronx. I got cut the first day. I can barely remember the tryout, honestly. I just remember it was during school, and I was embarrassed that I didn't make the team. Kareem did make the team, which ate me up inside. So, this was my very first crack at being on an actual Basketball Team. I picked the number 22 for some reason; not sure why, especially since Michael Jordan and Penny Hardaway were my favorite players at the time. I think it was just because the uniforms were based on size, and 22 was the best fit for me. I made it work.

That first game, I was a nervous wreck. I can't even remember who we played. I do know I had a hell of a game, though. I finished with about thirteen or fourteen points. We lost, but that game made everything click for me. That was the first time I felt fully accepted in North Carolina. The stares, the curiosity, and the questions all faded once people saw me play. Basketball translated in every language and every zip code.

But not everything I was learning in middle school was positive. Outside of the gym, I was picking up habits I shouldn't have. My Aunt, Cheryl Miller, originally from Detroit, taught me and my stepbrother, Maurice, how to steal. She didn't mind doing dirt, and even though her husband, Ed, didn't like it, he didn't stop her either. Their son, George, wasn't allowed to come, but Maurice and I started small. Little things from Food Lion or Walmart; candy slipped into jackets. Then it escalated: clothes, shoes, electronics... We felt like we were untouchable. That rush was real. We would sell stuff to our neighbors in West 22nd Street Apartments and made a killing doing it. At least, it seemed like that to us anyway. There were plenty of days we would walk to the local Food Lion, Shoe Show, or Walmart with hundreds of dollars in items. Some days, we would make two trips into the same store after dropping off items we had just stolen in a wooden area. We got caught at Big Lots in Kannapolis one day. The store called our parents. I remember that embarrassment clearly, but it didn't stop us right away. Sometimes, you learn lessons slowly.

Maurice had moved down from the Bronx to live with us after getting into trouble back home. His mom decided it was time for our dad to step up. Maurice fit right in with Mark, Ced, and Corey. He came down with a whole fresh wardrobe, and let me wear his clothes and shoes sometimes, which made me feel like one of the older guys. He wasn't much of an athlete, but he wasn't scared of anybody, and he could rap his ass off. After about a year and a half, our dad sent him back to New York. Not long after, he ended up in a group home.

Even though we had visited the South before, living there full-time was different. The dirt roads in Mooresville were long, dusty, and quiet. I'd walk to the bus stop and come home with dirt coating my shoes. Once we moved to West 22nd Street in Kannapolis, life felt more familiar—closer together, more noise, kids always outside. Families barbecued on porches. People hung out in parking lots. It felt more like a small version of the city. Family followed soon. My cousin, James, got a settlement for a slip-and-fall in New York, and used that money to buy land and a trailer in North Carolina. Joe eventually moved down, too. Having them around made me feel grounded. It brought a piece of the Bronx into our new life.

There were culture shocks that hit me hard. Seeing Confederate flags everywhere was something I had never experienced. I grew up around Blacks, Latinos, Whites… Everybody mixed together. In North Carolina, there were moments you felt the old South in ways you never expected. There was a trail behind our apartments that led to Rose Hill, and me, Ced, Mark, and other friends would walk it. The white owner of the land would threaten us with a shotgun, yell slurs like "nigger," and tell us to get off his property. That was one of the first times in my life I realized racism wasn't something you saw in movies; it was right there in front of me. But there were good parts too. The peace. The quiet. The safety. Not hearing gunshots. Not seeing drug deals. Being able to ride bikes without constantly looking over your shoulder. Neighbors like Vern, Cherita, Charlie, Sabetha, Shug, and so many others — we were all close, more like family than neighbors. That surprised me. I didn't realize how much noise I'd gotten used to in the Bronx until I finally experienced silence.

AAU with Dr. King changed everything for me. Dr. Allan King was tough—disciplined in a way that shaped me. His son, Drew, became family instantly. Our team had Jose Blackwood, who moved from Mooresville with his siblings. He lived in West 22nd also. He had a deep southern accent that cracked me up, but he was cool and could shoot. Max and Derek rounded out our group. We bonded fast because it felt like all of us were trying to find our place. He and I spent hours together playing games, shooting hoops, and just doing what kids our age in those communities do—getting into trouble. Ashley, Jose, and I once walked all the way from South Rowan to West 22nd Street because we couldn't get a ride. That had to be a five-plus-mile walk in the heat, but at that age, it didn't matter. We were young and free.

Practices were hard. Dr. King didn't play around. If you mouthed off, he checked you instantly. One day, I got too cocky and said something under my breath. He threw me out the gym. When I walked into the hallway still muttering, he kicked open the door and lit me up verbally. I needed that. Adults back then corrected you, and nobody ran to defend you. My parents didn't even blink when they heard about it.

My behavior had been slipping for a while in middle school: talking back, acting out, not doing my work, and just being a straight-up problem. During basketball season, I tightened up enough to stay eligible, always making sure I didn't cross the line, so I could practice and play. But by eighth grade, I pushed it too far. Everything caught up to me, and I ended up getting suspended near the end of the year. I remember being scared I might get held back. Back then, repeating a grade wasn't a sports tactic; it meant you failed. I passed my end-of-year tests, but that fear stayed with me. It was the first time I understood that the way I was acting could finally lead to a real negative consequence.

Basketball wasn't a priority, but it hadn't disappeared either. The sound of the ball hitting pavement or echoing in an empty gym was still familiar and comforting. I didn't know it then, but that small spark that hadn't burned out would end up finding its way back into my life. Everything after that was about to change.

Middle school taught me something I didn't even know I needed to learn: I could adapt to any environment. I could be the kid from the seventeenth floor of a twenty-story building in the Bronx, and I could also be the kid who said, "yes sir" and played Shelter Ball after school. I learned how to move between both worlds without losing who I was. But those same years also showed me how easy it was to make choices that could drag you in the wrong direction if you weren't paying attention. It forced me to grow up a little, and understand that my decisions could either push me forward or put me right back where I didn't want to be.

By the time I got to high school, I was already drifting away from basketball. My focus shifted to getting a job, making some money, hanging out, and doing the things most high school kids think about. I wasn't chasing the game the way I once had. I still played pickup here and there, but the fire had dimmed. Even so, something in me was starting to shift that summer before ninth grade. I didn't recognize it then, but there was a quiet pull in the background—something waiting on me, which I wasn't ready to name yet.

CHAPTER 3

FINDING MY WAY

High school at South Rowan hit me differently the moment I walked in. The hallways felt bigger, the voices louder, and the energy heavier. The older kids looked like grown men. The girls looked older than anything I was prepared for. Teachers moved like they had seen every type of knucklehead before and were already tired of us on day one. I had heard all the stories about freshman hazing: kids getting punched throughout the day, and seniors making ninth graders do stupid stuff. So, I walked in ready for anything. I really thought I would have to fight my way through the first few weeks. But it didn't happen like that.

South Rowan wasn't that big, and neither was Kannapolis. A lot of the upperclassmen already knew me. We had played pickup at local courts, rec centers, and YMCAs in Concord and Kannapolis. I had always hung around older kids growing up, so walking the halls with them around felt familiar, not intimidating. Whenever they saw me, they would just nod, "What's up, D?" It was simple, but it mattered. Being connected to guys people respected kept a lot of the nonsense off me. Even though South Rowan was a big 4A school with over 1,200 students, I never felt swallowed up by it. My transition was nothing like the horror stories. Before long, it felt like I belonged there.

I signed up for chorus with Ced, not because I thought I was some superstar singer, but because everybody said chorus was easy, fun, and full of the popular kids. That is where I met Mrs. Jan Gore. She was one of those teachers you never forget. Big heart, big smile, and a way of making you feel like you mattered, even on days you didn't feel like much at all. Chorus quickly became the one place where I didn't have to prove anything to anybody. Ced and I made Show Choir that year too. Antonio, Josh, Skip, and Ron were my guys. We stayed after school practicing, learning choreography, and trying to hit our notes without looking crazy on stage. We even did the Men in Black performance that had the whole auditorium hyped.

Antonio had one of the best voices I had ever heard: smooth, powerful, and controlled. I wasn't the best singer, but I could hold a tune, and I worked hard. And Mrs. Gore believed in me. When a few students could not attend All-State Chorus, she selected me to go. She did not have to choose me, but she did. That stayed with me.

She really poured into me that year, and throughout my entire high school career. When I eventually stopped singing, she was disappointed, but she understood that chorus had run its course in my life. I would still stop by her classroom from time to time just to say hello. By my senior year, when I had become one of the best players in the county, she would cut out newspaper articles about me and save them. She even bought me a photo album filled with pictures from both my chorus days and my basketball moments. I still have that album to this day. But at the same time, basketball was eating at me.

Freshman basketball was nothing like middle school. In middle school, I walked in and was instantly the best player. That confidence, maybe even cockiness, carried me everywhere. But freshman year humbled me fast. The freshman locker room was a different world. Freshmen were at the bottom, literally. JV and varsity got everything first: the best lockers, the best uniforms, the best schedules... the best everything. We got the leftovers: oversized jerseys that looked like they were from the early '90s, big shorts that didn't match anything, and a schedule full of whoever was willing to play us. We even played Jackson Training School, a school for kids with serious behavioral issues, because most high schools didn't bother having freshman teams, let alone scheduling them.

But I still thought I was going to shine. I thought my middle-school success would carry me right into this new world. It didn't. I wasn't ready. I didn't understand what real work looked like. I didn't understand conditioning, discipline, strength, or skill development. I definitely wasn't coachable either. I just assumed talent would carry me forever. Game after game, I sat on the bench. LJ and I were furious. We thought we deserved minutes because that is what we believed in our heads, not because of anything we had earned.

One game, the frustration boiled over. I hadn't touched the floor all night. Coach Swilley was coaching the rotation guys, and I sat there angry, embarrassed, and tired of feeling invisible. I waited until he turned his back. I grabbed my bag and walked into the locker room. Inside, Coach Parker, the long-time varsity head coach, was doing laundry. He looked up, confused, and asked what I was doing since the game was still going on. I told him I was quitting. He snapped back that I would never play for South Rowan again. I told him I didn't care because I wasn't playing anyway. Then I grabbed my stuff, walked out of the gym, and never stepped foot in it again for anything, except PE. I stopped going to games, stopped supporting the team, and stopped caring. I just changed out of my uniform, and quit mid-game.

I knew it was stupid as soon as I walked out the door, but pride wouldn't let me turn around. A week or two later, I saw Coach Swilley in the hallway. He looked disappointed, not mad. Somehow, that made it worse. I avoided him every chance I got. The funny part is he later put together a team for guys who played at Hall's Gym in Salisbury, and I ended up playing with Ced and Mark on it. We won a tournament, and I had some really good games. But even then, the spark didn't come back. And to this day, I still think walking away was one of the best things I ever did. I needed a break from basketball. I had fallen out of love with a game that once consumed me, and I needed time to figure out who I was without it. I needed space to grow, to mature, and to learn myself before basketball could ever mean anything again. Basketball faded out of my life for the next couple of years without me even realizing I had walked away from the very thing that would eventually give me everything.

My toughest basketball moment came early in high school when I realized I wasn't one of the best anymore. Players who used to be behind me had caught up; some had passed me. I wasn't focused, I wasn't working, and basketball wasn't at the front of my mind. I assumed I would always be better just because I had been before. Life doesn't work like that. The game doesn't work like that. If you don't keep evolving, you get left behind—and I did.

Years later, I would feel that same reality overseas in Romania. I had just replaced a player who was stranded with no flight home, no money, and no plan. And it hit me instantly: if they could do that to him, they could do it to me. After the success I had in Germany, I knew I belonged at the pro level, but Romania was the moment that forced me to prove it.

That game against Cluj was the turning point. One of the most fulfilling games of my entire career. It was the moment I earned my place, solidified myself as a real pro, and never looked back. When I think about all the guys I played with and against—high school standouts, college teammates, overseas pros—I rose to the top through a path nobody expected. That moment in Romania confirmed what I had always hoped was true: I had what it took. But back in high school, I didn't see any of that coming. Instead of stressing over basketball, I poured myself into other things. New people. New habits. A completely different lane.

Chorus kept me busy for a while, but the accident with Skip changed everything. One day, before show choir practice, me and Skip were riding around in the rain—music loud, windows fogged up, and just doing the kind of dumb stuff teenagers think is harmless. We had smoked a little. Nothing crazy, just the typical bad decisions kids make without thinking. We came around a curve too fast, hit another car, and ended up in a ditch. The sound of glass shattering, the crunch of metal, the truck tilting sideways—that noise still lives in my head. I climbed out of that truck alive, soaked and shaken, but something inside me shifted immediately. I remember standing there in the rain, thanking God out loud without even thinking. After that day, I drifted away from Skip. Ced did too. Life just pulled us in different directions. And that is when the "grown" version of my teenage years really started.

I got my first job at Chick-fil-A at fifteen, and suddenly, making money felt better than anything else in my life. Ced joined soon after. Reese helped both of us get hired. My sister or my dad would give me rides when they could, and when they couldn't, me and Ced would scrape together gas money for anybody willing to drop us off.

We worked a lot: nights, weekends, whatever shifts they handed us. And every single night before closing, we would drop extra chicken so we could take sandwiches and nuggets home. To this day, I still laugh about it, but the truth is that we were feeding our families sometimes. Ced and I always joked that we invented grilled nuggets before Chick-fil-A ever did. And the more hours I worked, the more I wanted to look the part. I was grabbing all the latest hip hop clothing and sneakers. Staying fresh was everything back then. I would spend whole paychecks on outfits, shoes, and anything that made me feel like I was leveling up. Eventually, I learned how to manage my money better. But in those early days, every new drop had my name on it.

Annette, our manager, eventually offered me a crew-lead position, but by then, I was ready for something different. I worked at Target during the holidays with my sister. Then I picked up hours at Pizza Hut, where I learned how to wash dishes fast, make pizzas, and bring food home like it was part of the job. None of it was glamorous, but it was money, and money meant freedom. And freedom became addictive.

We were always meeting girls at the mall, hanging out on days off, or killing time after shifts, since Chick-fil-A was in the mall. Basketball barely crossed my mind. On some Sundays, we would sneak into the Kannapolis YMCA to play. Those Sundays were packed—battles everywhere. My cousin, James, was living in Kannapolis then, and he would come hoop with us. Girls always had a thing for James. He was good-looking, smooth, and carried himself with confidence. We spent a lot of time together during those years. I would stay over at his and Joe's place on weekends. Joe always had the newest music, the newest game systems, and we'd spend hours just vibing.

I bought a pager. Then a prepaid phone where you had to buy minutes. I bought clothes, shoes, things I thought made me grown. I would walk into school thinking I had it all figured out. Really, I was just a kid trying to feel like something. Most nights, I ended up at West Green Apartments. Me, Ced, Mark, Loci, Rich, and 3, whose real name was Norwood would hang out, sometimes smoking, bringing girls over, and acting way older than we were. It wasn't every day, but it was definitely more than we should've been doing. West Green had its own energy: music playing from apartments, people on porches, kids running around, and everyone knowing everyone. It felt alive in a way I connected to.

Then there was the apartment of Tyleka, Ced and Mark's sister. She could cook anything: stir-fry hot dogs and sauerkraut... whatever she felt like throwing together. I thought it was five-star dining back then. She treated me like family; she let me stay there sometimes with Ced and Mark, laughing, talking, and clowning around. That place became a second home for all of us.

On weekends, we would ride around, hoop at different spots, hang at the Concord Mall, or hit The Gem Theater where movies were one dollar. On Friday nights, we would go watch A.L. Brown football games, mostly to see Nick Maddox, one of the best high school athletes in the entire country. But really, we were there to socialize, meet girls, and feel like we were part of something.

And the music... the music shaped us. Nas. DMX. Foxy Brown. Puff. Mase. Bad Boy had the whole world in a chokehold, and Jay-Z was becoming the greatest rapper we had ever heard. Those songs became the soundtrack to the versions of ourselves we were trying to become. Somewhere in that mix, I got my first tattoo—"Poppy," my nickname from New York. Eric did it with a needle, fire, and ink. It hurt like hell, but at fifteen or sixteen, that tattoo felt like armor. It showed just enough when I wore a jersey or short sleeves. I eventually covered it up years later, but back then, it was part of my identity.

All of this—the friends, the jobs, the late nights, the accident, the drifting—was shaping me in ways I didn't understand yet. Basketball was quiet during those years. It wasn't calling me. It wasn't pushing me. It was just... there. Waiting. Sitting in the background while I tried to figure out who I was without it. I didn't know then that the game wasn't done with me. I didn't know the fire was still there, buried under everything else. I didn't know I was setting the stage for the biggest comeback of my life.

All I knew was that I was a kid trying to find myself, through mistakes, growing pains, small victories, and stupid decisions. I didn't realize I was building the story I would one day tell. I didn't know the spark was coming. But it was. And when it finally hit? My whole life changed.

CHAPTER 4

THE SHIFT

Going into my junior year, life felt like it was slowly pivoting, even before I realized what was happening. I was still working shifts, running around with friends, and living like any other teenager who thought being grown meant having a little money in your pocket. But somewhere under all that noise, basketball started calling me back. Not loud at first; more like a steady nudge I felt when I walked past a gym or heard a ball bounce. I didn't know it yet, but that summer would change everything.

Freshman and sophomore years weren't basketball years for me at all. I was perfectly content working at Chick-fil-A, making money, hanging around West Green, or riding with Ced, Loci, Rich, or Reese. Basketball wasn't a priority anymore. I knew I could play, but I wasn't putting in any real work. Honestly, I didn't even understand what "work" truly meant back then. Skill development wasn't like it is today. There were no trainers or structured workouts. You just played pickup and hoped you got better.

Around that same time, life at home was teaching me lessons I didn't fully understand yet. When my mom was pregnant with my youngest brother, Bryant, she worked construction to keep us afloat, literally helping build the new additions to the apartments on West 22nd. I watched her wake up before sunrise, lace up her boots, work all day, and still come home to cook, clean, and take care of all of us. Seeing her grind like that, carrying a child and carrying a family at the same time, taught me everything about responsibility and resilience.

I didn't grasp the weight she carried back then, but now I recognize the strength it took. I can still picture her stepping off the bus after those long shifts—exhausted, but never complaining or quitting. She showed up every single day without excuses. That became the blueprint for me. Hard times don't last, but tough people do. And she was the toughest person I knew. She still is. Her example is the reason I move the way I do today.

But the spring before the school year ended, I found myself at the workouts Coach Parker was running for the basketball team. Something told me to go, even if I wasn't fully committed yet. me and Steven were in his PE class, and I think seeing us play against regular students made him raise his eyebrows a little. He could tell we had ability, even if we were still raw. Steve would attend some of the workouts, but I became a regular, slowly but surely. Steve just decided it wasn't for him; I kept at it though.

Those workouts were simple—conditioning, form shooting, footwork, plyo drills—but to me, they were the doorway back into something I thought I had walked away from. Drew, whom I hadn't been around in a long time, started hanging with me again too. He'd seen how much I had grown physically and kept pushing me to get serious, telling me the team was losing key players and they needed me. I didn't believe him at first, but he saw something I didn't. Carlos Dixon was the best player on the team my Junior year, and probably the best player ever to play at South Rowan. He would go on to play at Virginia Tech and overseas, like I did. He was a Senior, and most of the scoring left with him.

I had no idea what my role would be, but I knew just from workouts that I was going to be one of the top players. Now, to say I would have been the best, I would have been lying. I had lost my confidence along the way, and as a player, sometimes, it is hard to get back. I mean, playing pickup basketball and dominating, and playing in an actual game are two different things. I knew I had gotten better and could dominate at the local parks, recs, and YMCA's, but was I really as good as I thought I was? Then a wrench was thrown into my plan.

Coach Parker told us he would not be coaching anymore. I didn't realize how much I liked him until I saw the disappointment on his face. He was old school and sarcastic, but sharp. He believed in our potential long before we did. When he stepped away, Coach John Davis stepped into the head coaching job—the same man who once cut me from AAU and later swore he had never done it. When he asked me if I was going to play for him, I told him yes. I am not even sure if I fully meant it at the time, but saying it out loud made it real.

That summer was the first summer I ever truly worked at basketball. I was at workouts constantly, riding with Coach Davis or Drew whenever I needed a lift, doing whatever it took to get to the gym. When I wasn't there, I was hooping anywhere with a rim—Rose Hill, Bakers Creek Park, the rec center, open gym… it didn't matter. I would walk miles in the heat just to get shots up. That's when the game started to feel like home again.

Somewhere during that time, my body went into overdrive. I grew ten to twelve inches in what felt like a few months, but I didn't even notice it happening. All I knew was that I slept like I was hibernating and ate like every meal was my last. But people around me definitely noticed. Whenever I stepped into a gym or saw someone who hadn't seen me in months, the first thing I heard was "boy, you got tall." Dr. King said it with the biggest smile on his face, like he knew something I didn't. And Coach Parker didn't even recognize me when I showed up to his PE class. That's when it hit me: I looked like a basketball player now.

I had always been good, but now, the physical side caught up with the skill that was hiding underneath. I kept my guard skills even as I shot up to 6'6". I could dribble, finish, shoot, run—all the things smaller guards did—but now, I was doing it above defenders. The game slowed down for me. Moves that used to take everything out of me came easy. Confidence crept in quietly, but firmly.

Coach Davis noticed the change in me too. He didn't just become my coach; he became a mentor. After workouts, he would drive me home and talk to me about life, discipline, and responsibility; things I had never really heard from a coach before. Not long after, I met his wife, Kim. She was warm from the moment I stepped into their house. I think they both saw a kid with potential and pain, who needed direction, structure, and belief. They knew long before I did that I could be special if I stopped getting in my own way.

They welcomed me like one of their own sons. They fed me after practice, picked me up on weekends, so I could go watch Little John and Derek play in their football or baseball games, and always made sure I felt included. I loved spending time with them. At Christmas, they even made sure I had gifts under their tree. Their family became my family. Coach Davis' brother, David, gave me odd construction jobs to help me earn some money. And their father stepped in too; he helped me buy books during my first year of college. Looking back, their support carried me through some of the most important years of my life.

Not everyone made it through that grind unhurt. I remember one workout in the hallway where we were doing plyometric jumps, and my teammate, Jonathan Faggart, landed wrong and hurt his knee. He'd been MVP of JV for two years in a row and a returning varsity player. But I was getting too good to keep off the floor. I didn't say it out loud, but I knew it. Everyone did. The validation hit me during Catawba team camp. I wrote down every stat after every game like it was gospel: points, rebounds, assists, and everything. I dominated. That was the first time I saw real proof that the work mattered. That I wasn't imagining the rise. I finally believed I had something to offer the game, and that belief changed the way I carried myself.

But life doesn't move without interruptions. That same stretch when I was rising was the same time my father passed away unexpectedly. It was about two weeks before my senior year was set to begin, just after we had finished team camp at Catawba College. I remember my dad bursting into my bedroom late that night. I'm not even sure what he was looking for, but I was exhausted and annoyed. Not long after, my mom and sister woke me to tell me something wasn't right — he was acting strangely, and they were taking him to the hospital. That was the last time I ever saw him. One moment he was there, the next he was gone, and the news shattered the air in our home. My mom and sister came back from the hospital carrying a silence that said everything. It felt unreal, like time just paused around us. I didn't cry right away. I didn't know what to feel. I called John, and he came over immediately. He asked me what I needed, and the only thing I could think of was going to the gym at South and getting some shots up. I remember it like it was yesterday. I called John and he came right over end took me over to the gym to shoot. I turned the lights off and shot in the dark. Every shot echoed. I didn't count makes or misses. I just kept shooting because I didn't know what else to do. That night changed the way I approached everything. I stopped coasting. I stopped drifting. I stopped thinking like a kid. I told myself that if I was going to do this, I had to do it for him.

The season didn't start with fireworks. Four points in the opener against East Rowan. But I bounced back fast. Dropped twenty-one on North Rowan, one of the toughest teams around, then another twenty-plus against A.L. Brown. After that, everything clicked. Everyone in the county knew who South Rowan's best player was. And I stepped into that fully.

Then came the night that stamped my name into the record books. Northwest Cabarrus, the same team that had embarrassed us weeks before. I walked into that game with a different kind of energy. I knew nobody on that roster could guard me. I had already given them twenty-plus on their court. But that night, something else took over. When the game ended, I had forty points and twenty-two rebounds, breaking both school records. I didn't even know it until after. In the moment, you're not chasing numbers; you're just destroying whatever's in front of you. The next morning, Mike London from the Salisbury Post showed up at school with a box of Blow Pops and a notepad. When I saw my name in the paper, it felt like everything I had done in the dark finally showed up in the light. That season changed everything. It gave me purpose again. It gave me belief.

Losing my father sharpened my discipline. It made me think differently. I felt pressure to step up as a man; to help at home, to behave, and to think about my future. My siblings each dealt with it in their own ways. My mom was working constantly to support us. My sister helped raise Bryant and figure out her life. Brandon was finding his own lane. Looking back now, I realize that after my father's death, we all drifted, not out of love, but out of survival. I had basketball to keep me grounded, and was surrounded by people like John and Kim, Mrs. Gore, and Dr. King, who all believed in me when I didn't know how to believe in myself. My siblings didn't have that same kind of village, and I wish I'd been more present for them.

Academically, I was solid. Better than people might've expected from the kid who used to act out and get suspended. I had a new mindset: gratitude instead of entitlement. And people could feel it. John took Drew and me around to different college tryouts. My best showing was at Catawba, but their coach at the time, Jim Baker, said I'd need to go Juco first before giving me a shot with his team. They had a solid program for Division 2 and always recruited out of state, even overseas, instead of locally. Deep down, I believed that if I went Juco, I'd end up Division I without question. But something about that path didn't feel right.

I applied to Pfeiffer University and got accepted without even submitting SAT or ACT scores. Call it fate, call it timing, call it grace.... I went to their tryout and played one of the worst sessions of my life. The assistant coach, Rob Perron, told me they liked my game but couldn't promise me anything. That was enough for me. Senior year ended the way it was supposed to—with growth, clarity, purpose, and one final reminder of how far I'd come. I was late to my own graduation, running into the auditorium with Brandon Littlejohn as Mrs. Gore waved frantically, trying to make sure I didn't miss my moment. That was her: always looking out.

After graduation, I hit Myrtle Beach for a few days, pockets full of grad money, future full of possibility. A few weeks before college started, I officially signed with Pfeiffer. No girls holding me back. No distractions. No street stuff. No excuses. I walked into college a completely different person from the short, skinny freshman who quit basketball three years earlier. I had grown physically, mentally, emotionally, and spiritually. I had discipline. I had direction. I had purpose. Or at least I thought I did.

CHAPTER 5

FIRST YEAR AT PFEIFFER

Moving onto campus felt like stepping into another world. Pfeiffer was small and quiet, tucked into the woods about forty-five minutes from Charlotte, and thirty-five from Kannapolis. No traffic. No noise. No crowds. Just long walks between buildings, wide open fields, and a community where everybody already seemed to know everybody. Train tracks split one part of campus from the other, and every now and then, a train would crawl through so slowly it felt intentional—like it was daring you to try crossing. If you weren't already on the right side of the tracks, you were definitely going to be late to class or practice. For a kid who grew up in the Bronx and then Kannapolis, it was almost too quiet. Too slow. Too unfamiliar. It felt like the complete opposite of everything I had known.

I had just gotten my license, and I pulled onto campus in the 1987 Cadillac El Dorado my dad left me before he passed. Light brown with the leather top. The car was clean but unpredictable; it broke down on me more than a few times. Whenever it did, Mrs. Davis or my sister had to come get me on Fridays. Pfeiffer was only thirty-five or forty minutes from Kannapolis, but with everything I had been through, it felt like three thousand miles. Especially after losing my father just a year before.

Homesickness hit fast. Not the "I miss my bed" kind; more like the "I don't know if I belong here" kind. I didn't know anyone. I barely talked. Half the time, I went straight to my room after class, shut the door, and just sat there. My roommate, Wale, was an upperclassman—chill, respectful, always calm. He gave me space without making me feel weird about it. His girlfriend, Carrie, stayed over all the time. I didn't care at all; I spent most weekends back home anyway. I almost never stayed on campus that first year.

The dorm itself was simple—third floor, shared bathrooms I hated using, and showers that echoed every noise on the hall. I hated using the toilet so much I'd walk all the way to the library just to use a clean one. I kept microwaved food in the room so I didn't have to go to the café. And I had gotten my first credit card, which was probably a mistake. I ran it up fast buying food, games, and anything else that made the days pass easier.

Despite the isolation, I wasn't completely on my own. Coach Perron checked on me almost every day. He would pull me aside for one-on-one workouts and push me in ways I had never been pushed before. His sessions were no joke: back-to-the-basket work, drop steps, elbow jumpers, jump hooks, finishing everything high, and if I was anywhere near the rim, it needed to be a dunk. He was the first coach to drill that expectation into me. He believed in what I could become long before I did, and I found myself leaning on him more than I realized at the time. That preseason, before the season started, practices were intense. Pfeiffer had just won the conference championship, went 18–0 in conference play, and earned an NCAA bid. They returned the Player of the Year, Nem Sovic, and the best point guard in the league, Terrence "Tee" Baxter. Those dudes were different. Experienced. Confident. Tough.

I got told early I'd be redshirting—so would Rico, another freshman, and Joe Easley—and at the time, I took it the wrong way. I didn't understand that redshirting could've been the best thing for me. Instead of grinding harder, I shut down. I missed practices I should've been at, went home too much, and hid from the discomfort instead of learning to grow inside it. Rico didn't run from it. He showed up and made a name for himself. I didn't understand yet what real work looked like. Still, when I did practices, go to the gym and shoot or workouts, I showed flashes: my athleticism, my speed, and my ability to run the floor like a guard. But flashes weren't enough at this level. Not with a program this good.

And that's where the older guys came in. Terrence was lead point guard and Nem was the best player in the conference, and one of the best in the country. The guy could score with the best of them and could do it all. T-Bax was a super-fast point guard who was the engine behind the Pfeiffer system and led the conference in assist and steals. Nem would be named an All-American while T took home first team all-conference honors. I didn't watch many games that red shirt freshman year, but I do remember one in particular that I went to, and the basketball was amazing.

Even with the struggles, there were moments I'm grateful for. I earned Scholar-Athlete my first semester with a 3.0 GPA. That would be the last time my GPA was that high, but it meant something to me. It showed me I belonged academically even when everything else felt hard. During weekends, I'd go home, hang with my cousins, work for Mrs. Davis at her cell phone store, and sometimes, avoid thinking about basketball altogether. One Friday, she came to pick me up, and I finally said it: "I want to quit. Pfeiffer ain't for me." She lit into me. That conversation changed everything. She reminded me I was the first in my family to go to college. That people had sacrificed, supported, believed in me in ways I didn't always realize. Quit? After everything? From that day on, I never said the word again.

As spring workouts started, I came out of my shell a little. Began going to the café more. Joined the workouts again. Played in more open gyms. I slowly started to feel myself growing. I was becoming more confident and consistent. And there was a moment—one clear moment—when I finally thought: "I belong here." It was during offseason pickup when we were hosting recruits. I was scoring off the dribble, rebounding, guarding multiple positions, and running the floor better than guys older than me. The coaches pulled me aside afterward. That was the first time I felt like a real college player. Right before the school year ended, Coach Dave Davis called me into his office. He told me straight: "You can be a professional basketball player if you really commit. You've got the tools, but you need to lock in." I thought he was crazy. But he saw something in me I didn't see in myself yet. And that summer, I came back ready to prove him right.

CHAPTER 6

SOPHOMORE YEAR

That next year, I came back with something to prove. I earned a starting spot for the first two or three games. Our first matchup was against Catawba College. Myself and Rico Grier, a freshman point guard from Charlotte, were the only first-year players in the starting lineup. Rico was more outgoing and had been heavily recruited by Pfeiffer. T-Mac was around that year too—6'4", smooth as silk with the ball. A true point-forward. He could bring it up like a guard, post like a forward, score it from anywhere. Watching him taught me feel, pacing, and patience. Big Boy was older—about 25 or 26—and strong as hell. He took my starting spot early my active freshman year, and honestly, he deserved it. He was seasoned. He had grown-man strength and experience I didn't have yet. Those two showed me the difference between "talented" and "college-ready."

Catawba was a big deal to me because their coach had told me the year before that I'd need to go to junior college first before coming there. I always wondered if he had actually watched me play. He liked recruiting foreign players, probably because they were usually more polished at that stage. Either way, I had something to prove that night. We lost the game because they were more talented and experienced, but I had a solid showing with nine points, five rebounds, and a rim-rocking dunk that got the crowd on their feet. It felt good to make a statement. I don't think Catawba scheduled Pfeiffer again for a few years after that.

The next couple of games were rough, though. My production dropped, and I fell out of the rotation for a while. My confidence took a hit. But in college, nobody waits on you to feel better. It's about winning and staying locked in. Coach Davis cared about us, but he had standards; his last two teams were among the best in the country, and he wasn't lowering the bar for anybody.

I spent a good ten to twelve games watching from the bench, playing limited minutes. But late in the season, something clicked again. Over the last few games, I averaged double digits in three straight matchups and started finding my rhythm. I ended up averaging around five points and two or three rebounds that season in roughly nine minutes a game. At Pfeiffer, the system was built for speed and intensity. You went as hard as you could for two or three minutes, then the next five came in. Coach Davis designed that system himself. It was one of the first of its kind—full-court trapping, fast pace, and constant pressure.

That environment forced you to compete or get left behind. It also forced me to grow. I was learning what it really meant to sacrifice, to stay ready, even when it wasn't my turn, and to survive in a system that demanded everything from you. Players were constantly coming in and transferring out during my time at Pfeiffer. The program wasn't built for everyone, and honestly, I could have been one of the guys who left too.

We would see players around campus who had quit or were planning to leave, and it always felt strange. We all knew how hard it was to play for Coach Davis, and how much he expected out of you every single day. The guys who left didn't regret it; many of them went on to have solid careers elsewhere. But I like to believe the ones who stayed gained something deeper than minutes or stats. The years I spent at Pfeiffer made me tougher than I could have ever imagined. That toughness carried into every part of my life long after the basketball stopped bouncing. By the end of that season, I wasn't just a redshirt freshman anymore. I was part of something bigger: a culture built on work, discipline, and belief. I was a regular at workouts after the season, putting in real work on the weightroom.

That first year taught me that no one hands you anything, and that opportunity only comes to those who are prepared to meet it. And I was getting ready.

My sophomore year at Pfeiffer was special. Looking back, that might've been the most talented team I ever played on. We had dudes who could really hoop. Ray McKeithan was our best player: a 6'7" forward who could do everything. He was smooth, skilled, and confident, easily one of the most talented players I've ever shared the court with. me and Ray became close that season. He lived right across from my dorm, and we spent hours in his room playing video games, burning CDs with the latest music, or just talking about basketball and life.

That team was full of characters and talent. Rico Grier, our floor general, was a kid from Charlotte who could flat-out play. His younger brother, Demario, was coming up behind him and would become a great player in his own right, one of the most prolific scorers in Pfeiffer history. Kenny from Virginia was a walking bucket and one of the best pure scorers I've ever played with. Anthony Williams, who we called Gumby, was talented too, and was a key piece for us who could defend, rebound, and finish inside. Then there was Tim Granold, our best shooter from Germany, and James Johnson, who became a big influence on my development. James didn't just talk about hard work; he lived it. He'd drive me to summer-league games, where I played against other college players and even pros. Those games tested me, but they also gave me confidence. Playing in those runs showed me I belonged, that I could compete with anybody. Every game I could feel my growth.

We finished that season 22–9. We came up short of an NCAA Division II tournament bid after losing the conference-championship game to Belmont Abbey. That was a tough one, but it also lit a fire in us. It was the last time we'd lose to them. That same year, I had my breakout moment. We were playing Barton College, one of the best programs in the conference. I'd been working my tail off—extra shots, film study, weights, everything. When my number was called that night, I delivered. I finished with 18 points and 9 rebounds in limited minutes, and from that moment, everything changed. The next day, Coach Davis showed us film from that game. He paused one clip, pointed at me, and said, "That's an impact player right there." Hearing that from him meant everything. It validated the grind.

I was doing work-study at the time, grading film for Coach Hedrick. It wasn't glamorous, but it taught me a lot. My job was to double-check our stats after each game—points, rebounds, assists, turnovers—and make sure everything added up. I loved it because I've always been a stat guy. I wanted my numbers to be right, especially as my game started to grow.

That same season brought my first real taste of freedom too. After the year ended, me and Ray were supposed to go down to Florida for spring break with our friends, Katrina and Josie, who we'd gotten close to over the year. Ray ended up not being able to go, but I went anyway. That trip was unforgettable. Katrina took me home to meet her family, and they treated me like one of their own. We went to the beach, laughed nonstop, and for the first time, I felt what people meant when they talked about the "college experience." I actually had a crush on Katrina; she was a year older and dating a player from our JV team at the time. We, however, stayed cool and became good friends. That trip showed me there was more to college than just basketball, and it was one of those memories that stuck with me for years.

We had 6 a.m. workouts in the gym before the season, and those sessions were brutal. Coach Davis didn't play about being on time either. If you weren't at least ten minutes early, you were late. We'd be dragging ourselves in half-asleep, and he'd be there smiling, handing out honey buns, orange juice, Mountain Dew, and leftover Halloween candy like it was fuel. Somehow, we made it through. To this day, we still laugh about how we survived those workouts.

During the off-season in the fall and before the spring, we'd have more morning workouts and conditioning. In the afternoons, we'd usually have running, unless a "recruit" was visiting to play pickup. I use that word lightly. Sometimes, we'd get desperate and bring in just about anyone with a year of eligibility to save us from running. One time, we actually picked up some random guy at the local Wendy's and brought him to the gym to hoop with us. He played pickup, we avoided running, and everybody won. Not sure if other schools did stuff like that, but that's how we did things at Pfeiffer for sure.

Road trips were an adventure too. We usually took two vans. Coach Davis sat in the front with his little TV and VHS tapes, breaking down film by himself or pulling one of us up to watch for a few minutes. Meals were nothing fancy: Wendy's or McDonald's dollar menu, or Subway five-dollar subs. There was always a big cooler full of drinks: water, soda, and if we were lucky, some Gatorade. And you could count on there being bananas in there every single time. Home games weren't much different. We'd grab something from the café, then hit the local pizza spot right by campus after.

Rico's grandfather, Mr. Paul, was a legend in the Charlotte area for back when he hooped was a staple at Pfeiffer during our playing days. He and Rico's mom, Paula, were at nearly every game, cheering the loudest. Mr. Paul would hand a few dollars to the best players after each game, just to keep us with a little money in our pockets. Guess you can call it NIL before there actually was any. Haha. Paula would cook Thanksgiving dinner for the team during the holidays, and Mrs. Pam Davis, Coach's wife, did the same. Those little things made it feel like family.

That team had a bond. We pushed each other. We argued, competed, celebrated, and suffered together. One of my favorite memories from that year was when I rapped over the Jadakiss "Put Your Hands Up" beat in Tim's dorm room. He recorded it, and my teammates went crazy. They said it was one of the dopest things they'd ever heard. For that moment, I wasn't just a hooper; I was the team's entertainer too.

As much as I was growing as a player, I was also growing as a man, learning who I was and what I wanted. Around that time, I started dating Lauren, one of the stars of Pfeiffer's volleyball team. We started talking the summer after my sophomore year through AOL's AIM messenger and phone calls that went late into the night. She had originally been seeing Ray, but when he left school, we grew closer. By the time junior year rolled around, we were inseparable. I grew close to her family too, especially her mom, Lynn, and her sister, D.

Lauren was a good girl, and we had a strong bond. But as I got more success on the court, my focus started to drift. I was young, a college athlete, and attention came easy. I started talking to multiple girls, thinking that's just what came with the territory. I wasn't proud of that behavior then, and I'm definitely not proud of it now, but it's part of my story. I was growing, learning, and making mistakes, like most young men trying to figure out life. Going into my junior year, I was becoming a big man on campus. I knew everybody, and everybody knew me. We worked hard and partied even harder: local clubs, bars, and nights in Charlotte whenever we wanted a break from basketball. Those were some great times.

One person who made a huge impact on me that year was Coach Courtwright. He came in at the perfect time in my development. Coach Davis was intense, demanding, and set the standard. Coach Hedrick was detailed, fiery, and old-school. But Coach Courtwright was the balance we needed—steady, patient, encouraging, and the type of coach who talked to you in a way that made you feel seen.

He believed in me in ways I hadn't yet believed in myself. Anytime I asked him to rebound for me, he showed up. Early mornings, late nights; it didn't matter. His presence became part of my routine, my confidence, and my growth. I was already putting in the work, but having someone in your corner telling you that you're capable of more can change everything. And for me, it did. He never yelled or tried to be something he wasn't. He was calm, genuine, direct, bringing the exact contrast to the fire and edge that came from the rest of our staff. That balance made our team better, and it made me better. Even outside basketball, he and his wife were some of the kindest, most sincere people I had ever met. After that season, he moved on and eventually became a principal. Our time together at Pfeiffer was short, but the influence he had on me lasted long after he left. To this day, when I think about the coaches who shaped my journey, his name always comes to mind.

The café food I complained about as a freshman even started growing on me. I'd hit breakfast with Q, Gumby, and Tricky, and Miss Sue would make us omelets on mornings after workouts. That team was genuinely close, and I think that connection played a major role in our success. We opened the season with an 18-game win streak, shocking a lot of people. I think we were picked third or fourth in the preseason poll, and honestly, that made sense. Even though we returned almost everyone, losing Ray was huge. He would've been a preseason Player of the Year candidate without question. But looking back, I'm not sure we would've had the same chemistry had he stayed. That junior-year group was special; everyone worked, and the chemistry was undeniable.

Our first loss of the season came at Mount Olive. We had been trailing most of the game, but made a furious push late to tie it. I remember the final play like it happened yesterday. I was guarding the inbounder. He threw it to Marcus West at our free-throw line. Marcus turned and launched a dart toward their basket, almost a full-court heave, and somehow, it went straight in. At first, none of us believed it counted. We jogged upstairs to their locker room defeated, convinced we had just lost at the buzzer. Even the officials weren't sure. A few minutes later, they came upstairs to get us because they thought the shot might have actually missed and that we would be heading into overtime. For a moment, we felt a spark of hope. But after reviewing the video, the refs confirmed the shot was good. They beat us by three.

That walk back to our locker room was one of the most humbling feelings I have ever experienced. If that shot hadn't fallen—the miracle of all miracles—we knew we would have beaten them in overtime. We just had their number. To make it even crazier, that shot ended up No. 1 on SportsCenter's Top Ten. The only time we got national attention all year was for the one loss we took. For a long stretch, we were the only undefeated team in the entire country, regardless of division, but ESPN waited until we lost to highlight us. Still wild to think about.

By the end of my junior year, I was averaging 14 points in 20 minutes a game; right on pace for my goal of a point per minute, which Pfeiffer legend, Nem, had done years before. I knew the system worked if you committed to it. That season, everything clicked. We finished 31–3, winning both the regular-season conference title and the conference-tournament championship. I earned Second Team All-Conference, one of my proudest moments up to that point. Pfeiffer hosted the NCAA Division II East Regional in Mercer Gym, and the whole place was rocking. Charlotte news stations, local papers, fans from everywhere; that tiny town of Misenheimer had never seen anything like it.

We dominated the regional and punched our ticket to the Elite Eight in Bakersfield, California. For many of us, including me, it was our first time ever flying. Everything felt surreal—the travel, the hotel, the cameras, the feeling of representing something bigger than ourselves. In California, on the biggest stage we had ever played on, I put up 21 points and 5 rebounds against Kennesaw State in the Elite Eight. I played one of the best games of my college career, but it still wasn't enough. We lost by about eight points to the team that would go on to win the national championship. That one still stings. Kenny, our leading scorer all season, didn't hit a single shot that night. He had a complete meltdown and didn't even play the second half. And I believe to this day that if Kenny had been himself, we would have won it all. We had the team, the chemistry, and the momentum. We were the best squad in the country that year. No question.

After the game, we did interviews, went back to the hotel, and tried to process a season that had given us everything except the ending we wanted. When we finally returned to North Carolina, we hit a club in Salisbury and partied hard—part celebration, part heartbreak, and part release. It had been a special year, and I knew I had cemented myself as one of the best players in the conference. But I wanted more. I wanted to be one of the best in the entire country. As I've gotten older, I've realized that what's meant for you will find you. That national title wasn't ours to take, even though we believed we were ready for it. Looking back, that loss shaped me. It kept me hungry for whatever was coming next.

That season also gave me friendships and bonds that went beyond basketball. Qamar Hasan (Q) was one of the most talented players I ever played with. Injuries kept him from reaching his full potential at Pfeiffer, but anyone who saw him play knew how gifted he was. Q and Rick Buffaloe both looked out for me and a lot of the guys. They'd let us borrow their cars whenever we needed to run to the store, get a haircut, or just escape campus for a few hours.

Those little moments: the long road trips, the jokes in the locker room, the walks back from practice to our dorms, the late-night poker games, the inside jokes, the campus parties, the girls, and the random trips to other colleges just to hang out, all made that season unforgettable. It stopped being just about wins and losses. It became about brotherhood, growth, and getting ready for whatever came next.

CHAPTER 7

THE SUMMER BEFORE THE RUN

The summer before my senior year didn't start with hype. It started with responsibility. I found out I was one credit short of being eligible for the fall, so I enrolled in a class at Rowan-Cabarrus Community College. It wasn't glamorous, but it grounded me. Between summer school, basketball, and working camps, I had structure, and at that point in my life, structure was exactly what I needed.

Basketball never stopped. Me, Rico, and Mario kept our games sharp by jumping into every summer league we could find around Charlotte. Those runs were different. Former pros, college stars, grown men with real strength and real experience. Nobody cared about your school, your stats, or your reputation. You either produced or got exposed. Those games built my confidence. They showed me I could compete with anybody. Coach Davis also plugged us into something special. Through his friendship with former Pfeiffer coach, Bobby Lutz, now the head coach at UNC Charlotte, he connected us with their strength coach, Preston Greene. At the time, Preston was already one of the top strength coaches in the country. Years later, he'd help Florida win a national championship, but before the world knew his name, we were getting trained by him like professionals. His workouts were intense, disciplined, and smart. They reshaped both my body and my mentality.

I worked Pfeiffer's summer camps—team camps and individual camps—running drills, teaching kids, and staying around the game. I didn't realize it then, but those hot gyms were where BOBW really began. Teaching, leading, developing players... the foundation of everything I do now started right there. I worked team camps at UNCC too, often officiating games. We'd make about $200 a camp, which felt like a lot back then. As I got older, I realized it wasn't, but at the time, it helped me stay afloat.

Off the court, life was complicated. I was still with Lauren, but we had our issues because of my immaturity. I made mistakes. I wasn't always doing right by her, but she stuck by me. Her mom, Lynn, and her sister, D, treated me like family, and I always appreciated that. Relationships at that age can be messy when you're still figuring out who you are. We actually broke up briefly in our senior year after I cheated, but we ended up getting back together before the season started.

That summer was a mix of growth, responsibility, mistakes, and maturing. I was getting stronger in every way. I was learning discipline. I was starting to fully understand what the game could do for my life if I treated it with respect. I played a lot of pickup at local parks, always showing why I was becoming a standout college player. Ced and I still hung out from time to time, and even though everyone was going their own direction, we always reconnected on the court when I was home.

I spent a lot of time with John, Kim, and their family too, going to their summer AAU games or just kicking it at their house. Coach Davis would throw steaks on the grill, or Mrs. Davis would make baked BBQ chicken. That home became a safe space during those years. I also played a lot of pickup at the YMCA in China Grove. People were shocked at how much better I had gotten. One guy who really tested me was Justin Pauley. He had been the only freshman to play varsity at South Rowan my freshman year and made All-County and All-Conference before moving away. He came home for the summer from his college, and I hadn't seen him in years. He knew I was a different player, but I think he still wanted to see for himself. We played one-on-one, and I beat him. I wasn't the 5-foot-6 freshman he remembered; not even close.

By the end of the summer, I felt a shift. I wasn't the unsure freshman. I wasn't the raw sophomore. I wasn't just the breakout junior. I was becoming a leader. A man. Someone ready for a defining season. Going into my senior year, I felt different. The foundation was set. The hunger was real. And for the first time, everything I had worked for felt like it was coming together. Now, it was time to finish the job.

CHAPTER 8

THE RUN

Senior year hit different from the start. I was finally living in the New Dorms; they were still being called the New Dorms nearly twenty years later, which is crazy. I had two new teammates as roommates: Rusty Kiddoo and Matt Austin. Even though Rick didn't officially live there, he might as well have. Both Rusty and Matt had transferred in from junior colleges. The setup was perfect: each of us had our own room and bathroom with a shared living room and kitchen. We even had a washer and dryer, which meant teammates and friends were always dropping by to wash clothes, grab snacks, or just hang out.

Rusty was the responsible one in the group—steady, organized, dependable—but he had his fun too. We constantly messed with him, putting random stuff in his room or making his bathroom the go-to spot during parties. Matt had that big personality that made everyone feel welcome: charming, good-looking, and a straight-up girl magnet. And then there was Rick, who was basically the fourth roommate. If he wasn't in our apartment, he was somewhere on campus playing poker or tearing up Taco Bell. We joked nonstop, roasted each other daily, and never took life too seriously. The things that happened in that apartment could fill another book. I still remember the superfan girl who had a huge crush on Rusty. She bought us a stereo system out of nowhere. She used to bring us snacks too. College life was wild.

On campus, we partied hard. The New Dorms were the spot, especially our place. Some nights, it felt like half the school was packed inside our living room—music blasting, drinks flowing, people watching games or just vibing. One afternoon in the café, Matt even invited some of the cafeteria workers to a party, and they actually showed up. We hooked them up with drinks and partied with them, the whole night. Even with all the fun, I stayed locked in. Nothing was going to get in the way of what I had worked my whole life to accomplish.

We started the year with those early-morning 6 a.m. workouts. You had to be there at least ten minutes early or you paid for it. Once preseason scrimmages were done, the season kicked off. Rico was coming off a First Team All-Conference season and had finished runner-up for Conference Player of the Year. He was our leader on the floor, but I was right there with him. Our games complemented each other perfectly. He controlled the tempo and put people in the right spots, and I was the forward who could score from anywhere. We didn't hang out as much socially that year, but we were still close. We'd hit Applebee's from time to time or shoot pool and get wings at Sharky's. Staying connected mattered, and I believe our chemistry played a huge part in our success. Most of my time was spent with Matt, Rusty, and Rick though. They were my everyday crew who made that year feel like something special on and off the court.

I came into my senior season about one hundred points shy of one thousand for my career. I hit that mark by the fourth game. The game slowed down for me in a way I had never felt. I was confident, in control, and locked in. I had nights where I was automatic, scoring twenty five, twenty seven, thirty, even thirty five points, all in under twenty minutes of playing time. But the season didn't start smooth.

We opened at 2–3. A lot of teams would have panicked, but not us. We had a winning culture. We trusted the work. And once we settled in, everything clicked. We went on a fifteen or sixteen game winning streak, and suddenly, Misenheimer felt like Misenheimer again.

We owned the Carolina–Virginia Athletic Conference during that era. Mount Olive was our toughest rival, but they still couldn't beat us. We added new pieces that year: Dele, Todel, Jason, and Craig. And Mario was coming into his own, consistently scoring in double figures and anchoring our second group. Dele was the perfect complement to Rico, running the point whenever Rico wasn't on the floor. Matt backed me up at forward and became one of our better defenders. We didn't look as intimidating on paper as we did the year before, but with me and Rico leading the way, we knew we had a chance to win every single night. Rico had this unwavering confidence that spread through the entire roster. I kept working every single day; by that point, I had become nearly unstoppable.

There were plenty of funny moments along the way too. Brad, our freshman, was always cracking jokes. On one road trip, Coach Davis said the word "cheeseburger" completely wrong. Brad repeated it exactly the way Coach said it, and the entire van exploded in laughter. Coach slowly turned around and told Brad that if he kept it up, there'd be a 6 a.m. workout waiting. The van went silent instantly. We still laugh about that moment.

I earned First Team All-Conference, First Team All-Region, and All-American honors. I won Conference Tournament MVP. Rico won Conference Player of the Year. At first, I was frustrated; I led the league in scoring and led our team in both scoring and rebounding, averaging 20.1 points and 5.8 rebounds per game. But as I've gotten older, I realized something that what is meant for you is meant for you. That award simply wasn't mine to have. And that's okay.

We hosted the East Regional again as the number one seed, and fully expected to return to the Elite Eight. Mount Olive was in the bracket, and we were ready for them. But basketball doesn't care about your expectations. We lost in the second round to Salem International—a team later found to be using ineligible players. Mount Olive went on to win the East Regional in our gym. We finished 28–5, a record most programs would celebrate. But at Pfeiffer, it felt like a disappointment. Especially knowing that Mount Olive won the regional, and we were confident we would have beaten them again. Like I've said before, sometimes, it's just not meant to be.

I didn't attend any of the remaining games after we lost. I was disappointed, relieved that the grind was finally over, and honestly shocked that our season ended the way it did. It took time to accept. My spring internship was at the local hospital with attorney Ron Burris. He was sharp, respected, and treated me with so much professionalism. I would file papers for him. Around that time, I, Rusty, Matt, and Rick met Emily, who played basketball at Duke. One night, the four of us drove up to Chapel Hill to watch the national championship game in the Dean Dome. Carolina won it all that night, and thousands of students and fans poured into the streets to celebrate. Ali, Emily, and a few of their teammates met us on Franklin Street, and people recognized them immediately. Carolina fans were giving them all kinds of grief—the usual Duke jokes—but they took it in stride and laughed it off.

A few weeks later, we went to Duke to hang out with Emily and Alison during Duke's end-of-year celebration. They took us inside Cameron Indoor, and I, Matt, and Alison ended up playing H-O-R-S-E under those historic rafters. The campus was wild that night—music everywhere, people partying in every direction. We stayed out way too late and didn't head back to Pfeiffer until the early morning hours.

I figured I could squeeze in a couple hours of sleep before my internship. Instead, I overslept horribly. I woke up in a panic, grabbed Rusty's car, and sped to the hospital. When I walked in, I found out the office had planned a surprise going-away party for me. And I had missed the entire thing. They laughed about it later, but in that moment, I felt terrible.

I wasn't perfect in the classroom either. Biology had been my struggle since freshman year. I failed it twice before finally passing it as a senior. Before the fall semester even started, I met with my professor and told him I would do whatever it took to pass. I meant every word. I knew that class was the only thing standing between me and my degree. Even though I wanted to play professionally and opportunities were starting to come, I wasn't leaving Pfeiffer without graduating.

After the season ended, I spent long hours in the library creating highlight videos to send to overseas agents. I knew Division I players usually got the first looks, but I trusted something would come if I stayed patient. And eventually, it did; my first offer came from the Newcastle Eagles in England. The one science class that had given me trouble for years finally fell into place. I earned the grade I needed, and with it, I secured my graduation. I was going to receive a college degree, being the first person in my family to do so. It was one of the proudest moments of my life.

The people who had always been there showed up that day in May: my mom, Tanya, Brandon, John and Kim, and even Mrs. Gore. Seeing them all in the crowd made the moment feel even bigger. By the time I graduated, I had accomplished more than I ever imagined as that skinny freshman who once walked away from basketball. I had found my voice, earned respect, and turned myself into a professional-level player. My time at Pfeiffer shaped me. It sharpened my mentality, humbled me when I needed it, and built a fire in me that still burns. And now, everything I had worked for was leading me to a new chapter. A new country. A new challenge. A new version of myself. The professional journey was finally about to begin.

CHAPTER 9

THE EUROPEAN GRIND

I spent that summer at home the same way I had the ones before it—working out, working camps, and playing in summer leagues. But if I'm being honest, I had taken my foot off the gas a little. Coming off an All-American season, I let myself believe I had "arrived." I wasn't lazy, but I lost sight of what had gotten me there in the first place.

I worked a summer camp at a YMCA in Charlotte as a counselor, and all the while, I waited for the right overseas offer. May passed. Then June. By July, I was getting nervous. I hadn't heard anything from my agent, Fred Besso, a French agent I had chosen to represent me. The overseas process is pretty standard: after the NBA Draft, teams start signing import players. Division I guys go first, then Division II, and so on. I knew my résumé and game film were strong, so I tried not to panic. Still, the silence was tough.

Then, in mid-July, the offers finally came. One of them was from the Newcastle Eagles in England. The moment I saw it, I knew it was the right first step. I officially signed my first professional contract with the Eagles. A couple of weeks before I was supposed to leave, I, Matt, Rusty, and Rick took a beach trip. While we were out in the ocean, I stepped on a seashell and sliced the bottom of my foot badly. For a moment, I really thought that injury might cost me everything I had worked for. But after about a week and a half, it healed enough for me to move around again. The only downside was I couldn't really work out those last couple of weeks before leaving.

When the summer ended, it was time to step into the next chapter of my life. My mom, Lauren, John, and Kim drove me to Charlotte Douglas Airport. I'll never forget signing my very first pro contract at Mrs. Davis's cell phone store on the way there. That little shop in China Grove held so many memories, and now, I was standing in it, making the biggest decision of my life. The entire ride to the airport felt surreal: exciting and terrifying at the same time. My mind kept drifting to the unknown ahead of me, wondering if I was really ready for this next step.

By the time we pulled up to the terminal, my palms were sweating. Saying goodbye wasn't easy. Pride, fear, sadness, and excitement all rushed in at once. It felt like the moment I had been chasing my whole life, yet somehow bigger than anything I had ever experienced. I knew I was going to miss my family, Lauren, the Davis family, and all my friends. I had never been away from anyone for more than a few weeks, if that. And I had definitely never flown that far on my own. California had been my first flight anywhere, and now, I was traveling across the ocean to another continent.

There wasn't a single person I knew personally who had ever done what I was about to do. I had heard stories here and there, but no one in my immediate circle had ever gotten the opportunity to play professionally overseas. I was stepping into a completely new, uncharted territory for me and everyone I loved.

I checked my bags, hugged everyone tight, went through security, and found myself sitting at the gate with a laptop, PSP, and MP3 player—

my only sources of entertainment for the trip. I stared out the window wondering if I was really ready for this next step. But there I was, ticket in hand, headed overseas to play professional basketball for the Newcastle Eagles. A dream realized. A life about to change.

Fab Flournoy, the head coach and a player for Newcastle, picked me up from the airport. The culture shock hit immediately. They drove on the opposite side of the road, the steering wheel was on the opposite side of the car, and everything felt backward to me. Fab was driving a team-sponsored car wrapped in Newcastle Eagles branding, and it all felt unreal; exciting, but strange.

He took me to grab some food, then to my apartment, and finally, to the team office to meet everyone. The accents threw me off at first. They understood me, and I understood them, but everything just sounded different. Everyone at the office was welcoming though. They gave me a prepaid phone with minutes, so I could call home and let my family know I had arrived safely.

We stopped by the gym next. Practice was already in full swing, so Fab told me to just watch and relax after the long flight. When it ended, I finally got to meet the team. Most of the guys already knew who I was. Fab had been raving about me for weeks, but even with that, I felt uneasy. New country, new system, new expectations... I didn't know how I'd fit in, on the court or off.

The team was coming off winning both the league championship and the cup. They had a long history of dominance, and everyone expected them to repeat. I came from a winning program too, so I knew what it took to win, but that was college. Winning overseas was different. More physical. More mental. More pressure. A lot of variables were in play, and I found myself wondering quietly if I was really ready for this.

One of the first players to make me feel at home was Charles Smith. He was one of the key guys on that roster. He was talented, respected, and a big part of why the Eagles were so successful. From day one, he welcomed me with open arms. He had watched my film, believed in my game, and made it clear he was excited to have me there. Even after everything that would happen, and after I left, Charles and I stayed cool for years. He was one of the real ones.

After that, he took me to a local fish-and-chips spot to grab more food, then by the grocery store for snacks. The team gave me a little money in case I needed anything else, and I went back to my apartment, opened my laptop, and called Lauren and the Davis family. I tried to sound confident and reassure them that I was good and ready for the challenge. But deep down, I wasn't. Mentally, I wasn't settled at all.

The very next morning, bright and early, Fab came to pick me up. They wanted to see exactly what I had. And I got exposed immediately. I was out of shape. I got bumped around. I was playing against grown men with strength and experience. That first practice humbled me fast. I got my ass kicked. I walked back into my apartment embarrassed, discouraged, and questioning everything. Being an All-American didn't mean anything there. That title held no weight in a gym full of pros.

A couple days passed, and the feeling didn't go away. It got heavier. After talking with Lauren and my family, I made up my mind. I wanted to go home. When I finally told Fab I wanted to go home, he wasn't mad; just irritated. And honestly, I understood why. They had invested in me, believed in me, and expected me to help them win. But my mind was made up. Before I left, I said goodbye to Charles, the one guy I had already built a small connection with, and to Nick, the other American import. Nick was also an All-American, coming out of a Division I program in Florida. We connected early on

68

because we were both navigating the same culture shock, expectations, and pressure. I later found out he ended up getting cut that season too. The team booked my flight, and just like that, I was back in the States.

What made the whole thing even crazier was that we had a game the very same day I left. My friend Dawn, who I knew from college, was in England at the time, coaching lacrosse. She had been homesick too, and we had emailed back and forth about meeting up. She took a long trip up just to watch me play and see a familiar face. When I got home, I opened my email and saw her message. I felt terrible. In the chaos of everything—the stress, the fear, the disappointment—I completely forgot she was coming. Thankfully, she understood. She always had a good heart.

I stayed with Lauren and her mom in Mooresville. I kept to myself, thinking about everything. It felt too familiar, just like when I almost quit my freshman year of college. I thought I had grown beyond that. But there I was again. After about a week, I knew I needed to give this another real chance.

Fred eventually secured me a contract in Germany with the Cuxhaven BasCats in the second league. With a new mindset and a chip on my shoulder, I got back on a plane and headed across the water again, this time, determined to finish what I started. Once I truly commit to something, I don't stop until I reach the goal. And this wasn't just about proving I could play overseas. This was about proving it to myself.

Germany welcomed me with cloudy skies, cold air, and steady rain. Cuxhaven was a small, quiet town right on the North Sea: a completely different world from England or anything I had known. The club director met me at the airport and drove me to a hotel near the water, where I'd stay until my apartment was ready. There was no internet in the room, so I had to walk to a small café anytime I wanted to Skype home or listen to music. It wasn't glamorous, but I was there with purpose. I knew why I came. And this time, I wasn't running from anything. I was running toward something.

We had another American named Kevin Martin. Big, strong dude from Florida who could defend, rebound, and finish around the rim. We had Lee Jeka, Benas Matkevičius, and his father, Coach Matkevičius, running the team. Janis, a young German player, became my guy. He drove me everywhere: practice, grocery store, metro. All of it.

My very first game: 26 points and 13 rebounds against one of the league's top teams. I averaged 18 points and 9 rebounds in Germany, both top ten in the league. Life was good. I had fans. I signed autographs. I was getting used to this pro lifestyle. One night we beat a first division team in the German Cup and all went out to Bremerhaven to party. Techno blasting, the lights wild, people staring at me and Kevin because we were the only two Black guys in the whole club. Kids shouting rap lyrics at us. It was crazy.

After a few months, I was really settling into life in Germany. Janis and I shared an apartment with reliable internet, and he had a car, so he drove us to and from practice and anywhere else we needed to go. We ate most nights at the team's sponsored restaurant; always a soup, a salad, and a main course. Usually fish. On rare days, we'd get chicken or beef. I didn't eat pork, so the chef always made sure to put something different together for me. When we didn't eat at the team restaurant, we cooked for ourselves. Mostly tacos—simple, good, and quick. On game days, I'd walk to the arena with my headphones on, locked in. As I got closer, I could always see a line forming outside. Little kids would run up asking for autographs. Sometimes, it was the exact same kids from the week before, but it never mattered. We thought it was cool every single time.

I became a gym rat again. After practice, I always wanted to stay and get extra shots or work on something to sharpen my game. Everyone has their own routine—their own way of putting themselves in the best position to perform. Mine was simple: outwork everyone. That mindset gave me confidence, and more importantly, it worked.

On off days, when the coach told me to stay out of the gym, I'd walk into town, shop a little, grab food, or just explore. I, Janis, Benas, and Kevin hung out a lot outside of practice, listening to music, burning CDs and movies, and playing games. Kevin stayed to himself more than the rest of us, but he was cool.

And on the court? I was dominating, finding my rhythm, and getting used to the lifestyle of an overseas pro. Everything was clicking. Until life did what it always seems to do: threw a wrench right into the middle of my plans. But overseas basketball is a business. About a week before Christmas, the club director knocked on my door. They were releasing me. I thought he was joking at first. He wasn't. They replaced me with an older fan-favorite player who had become available. It didn't matter that I was averaging 18 and 9; they made a business move. I packed my bags.

The bright side was I had money saved up. I went home, spent Christmas with family, and didn't stay unemployed long. Fred got me a better contract in Luxembourg for almost double the money. I took it. Luxembourg was rough from the moment I arrived. Seventeen hours of travel, an eight-hour layover in England. By the time I landed, I was exhausted. But the club director picked me up from the airport, took me straight to the apartment, and immediately asked if I could practice. No rest. No recovery. Just, "Can you go right now?" That's life overseas: produce or go home.

I went to the gym, stretched a little, and jumped straight into drills and live play. The moment I touched the ball, I knew I could dominate the way I did in Germany. These guys couldn't guard me. Fred had already told me they were a middle-of-the-pack team looking for an American who could score and rebound—my specialties. And for a while, I was doing exactly that.

Then, forty minutes into practice, I pulled my hamstring—bad. The next day, Fred emailed me. They were cutting me. They couldn't wait for me to heal. Just like that, it was over before it even started. But Fred already had another deal cooking. Romania. And Romania would change everything.

Sibiu, Romania was electric. The GM picked me up, took me to get phone minutes, food, and dropped me at the hotel where housekeepers did laundry for a few dollars. The city had energy. And my teammates, Darnell "D" Clavon, Brian Evans, and Brice Kabengele, became brothers instantly. D and I bonded over Dave Chappelle jokes every day.

I was still recovering when I arrived, but the coach and GM already knew that. According to Fred, they were willing to be patient. Patient in Europe must have a different definition though, because they asked me every single day how I was feeling, how long it would take, and when I could play. Little by little, I worked myself back in. At first, it was just light ball-handling and shooting. I didn't want to push too hard and risk a setback. Then I eased into some 1-on-1, then into running sets and drills with the team. The guys could tell right away that I could play, and that I was exactly the piece they needed, but I still wasn't close to fully healthy.

In my first game, I tried to give it a shot. I scored a modest eight points, and I could tell immediately the coach wasn't impressed. He didn't speak English, but his body language said everything. The smiles and laughs he had early on were Gone. And the fan page lit me

72

up after the game, saying that the club wasted time bringing me in, and that they needed a new import immediately.

I had told the coach I wasn't healthy, but I also knew that if I didn't play, he would've been even more frustrated. My second game was against the best team in the league: Cluj Napoca. The coach brought me off the bench, probably not expecting much. My teammates didn't know what was coming either, and neither did their fans. But that night, everything clicked. Off the bench, I exploded for 25 points and 12 rebounds, including a filthy crossover into a dunk that had the whole gym buzzing. Everything changed after that game. I went on to average 17 points and 10 rebounds that season. We made the semifinals and won bronze. All four Americans on our team made the All-Star team. Romania had turned into another chapter of proving myself, and rising again.

The crowds were insane. A couple thousand every game, standing room only. Guards with machine guns lined the court. Romania became home. Again, fans would line the gym before the game and greet us as we entered the arena. This was truly one of the best experiences as far as fans I had as a pro. It seemed like every home game, the entire city would shut down just to watch us play.

Nightlife in Romania was wild. We played hard, but we partied even harder. After wins, our coach would slide us bonuses—an extra thousand here and there. I'd send most of my money home and keep the bonus for spending. I, D, Brian, and Brice were inseparable. Anytime we had free time, we were together, enjoying the overseas life. Even on away trips, it was nothing for us to sneak out after team dinner and explore whatever city we were staying in. We always kept it cool though, never too crazy, and we always handled our business on the court.

D had a car, so he became the unofficial chauffeur, driving us to the store, McDonald's, or anywhere else we needed to go. He was my guy. We laughed constantly, watched old episodes of Chappelle's Show and Martin on repeat, and usually, if you saw him, you saw me. He definitely took me under his wing. We stayed close even after Romania. I visited him one summer in Atlanta, and we had a blast. Brian and Brice were my guys too. Brian was one of the best point guards I ever played with—dude could flat out play. Brice, from France, was crazy athletic and could shoot the air out of the ball. That group made Romania unforgettable.

Before my Cup game, I caught an elbow in practice; blood everywhere. I snapped and walked out. The GM got me stitched up and asked if I could still play on TV the next night. Of course, I played. We lost, but I had 17 and 10 on national television. We had made it all the way to the semifinals, which meant a long, exhausting season. Our run ended in the final game of the semifinals, losing to Cluj by one point—a brutal way to go out. Because of league rules, we still had to stay and play the bronze-series. None of us wanted to keep going after such a long year, but we locked in, swept the series 2–0, and took home the bronze.

After the season ended, we chilled for a few days while management finalized our last payments, booked our flights, and wrapped everything up. I went into the coach's office to get my final check, and I told him and the GM that I was open to coming back if the offer was right. They assured me they'd put something together that would make it worth my time. But I knew how overseas basketball worked. Most teams try to bring you back as cheap as possible. And I already knew they couldn't afford to keep all four Americans. All of us wanted raises, and all of us had strong seasons. They made their offer. And then came my moment of clarity.

I left that season with an offer to return, but by then, Fred had already sent my film all over Europe. I had options. I already had teams offering double what Romania had paid me for those five or six months. So, declining their offer wasn't difficult professionally, even though I had real love for the people there. I appreciated everything they'd done for me. We stayed on great terms. To this day, I, the coach, and the GM still keep in touch. Romania gave me growth, confidence, and a reminder of the kind of player I could be. But it was time for the next step.

Next stop: Czech Republic, Usti nad Labem. A stronger league, tougher competition, and a completely different environment. Usti was a small town about an hour's drive from Prague, the capital of the Czech Republic. When I arrived at the gym, the first person I met was Tim Henry, one of our American imports. Seeing another American is always a relief overseas; it gives you something familiar to hold onto. We clicked right away. His wife, Ashley, was cool from day one too.

They lived about a block from me, and we looked out for each other. We made trips into town together, rode the bus together, and grabbed groceries together, because when you're in another country, especially as Americans, you never quite know what to expect. People minded their business, for the most part. And if you minded yours, nobody bothered you. But those stares on the bus or in stores were real. They always knew we weren't from there. Most people were kind, but every now and then, a younger kid, trying to imitate lyrics from rap songs, would say the N-word. I always made sure to correct them respectfully. Most of them genuinely didn't understand the weight of the word.

Usti had its spots we came to love. The local bowling alley had surprisingly good food, and there were a few restaurants in town we hit regularly. The team covered meals from time to time too. Living there was cheap, and even without a car, public transportation made everything easy. Tim and Ibecame a solid one-two punch. Crowds packed our games. Kids chased us down for autographs. Payments were sometimes late—that's overseas ball—but they always came. As long as your money hits, you breathe easier.

That season, I met Levell Sanders, a Brooklyn guy who played for Decin and had carved out a long, respected career in the Czech league. We played against his team in the third or fourth game of the season, and I had a big night. After the game, he asked if I wanted to grab a bite, drove us to McDonald's, and we spent hours talking hoops and New York. Levell looked out for me that entire year. On his days off, he'd come to Usti and we'd hop in his car and ride to Prague—sightseeing, eating, catching movies, shopping. Prague became one of my favorite cities in the world. There was always something going on. Some Saturdays, we'd hit clubs after games. Other nights, we'd catch concerts. When Mobb Deep performed in Prague, I, Levell, and his teammate, Peter, were there front row.

Levell had a young friend named Eric (we all called him E); an African kid who lived in Usti, spoke fluent Czech, and seemed to know everybody. If E was with us, something hilarious was going to happen. He was that type of dude.

During the season, Matt came to visit with Sonya and a couple friends while they were backpacking through Europe. Matt was working at the airport at the time and could fly for free. Always down for an adventure, he landed in Europe and took the train straight to Usti. They came to the game the next day and watched me drop 25 and 10 in a rare win. We celebrated by heading to Prague and clubbing all night. One of his friends got so drunk he disappeared, and we didn't find him until the next day.

Our team in Usti was solid talent-wise, but not built to make a real run. me and Tim put up good numbers, but numbers don't always equal wins. The main goal every year for that club was simply staying in the top league, and we did that. A new GM came around that season: an American guy named Luther. He was Black, charismatic, and seemed cool, but something always felt off about the way he talked about the "drastic changes" he wanted to make. He insisted they'd pay more if me and Tim came back the next year. I was curious. Tim wasn't. With Ashley pregnant and his passion for the game fading, he was ready for the next chapter. He retired to go to law school, and he's a successful attorney now. We're still cool to this day.

Around that time, Levell introduced me to his agent, Bob Stanley, a staple in the Czech Republic, and especially connected to the top teams. Bob told me Decin was very interested in me and planned to make a strong offer. I told him I needed to clear my head, get home, and think about it. When I got home, I opened Eurobasket one day and saw it: Damien Argrett—MVP of the League. I averaged 20 points and 7 rebounds, and absolutely dominated the competition that year. It was the season where everything slowed down for me: mentally, physically, and rhythmically. I felt in control. Usti had been another step forward. And now, I had earned my way into the better leagues in European basketball.

I signed with Děčín that summer, and even negotiated a small signing bonus—nothing huge, just a couple thousand to get me through the summer. Levell had taught me that if a team truly wants you, you can ask for more. And they wanted me bad.

Bob told me Levell was leaving Děčín for a better contract elsewhere, which meant they needed a new point guard. The first person I thought of was my guy, Rico. Once Pavel, the head coach, saw Rico's video, and offered him on the spot. I was hype. Having one of my best friends with me in the same country and on the same team, felt surreal.

We trained all summer—workouts, pick-up runs, summer league—preparing for the year ahead. Rico fully trusted me on everything: the Czech league, the lifestyle, the basketball. He was all in. We left in August and made that long overseas trip together for the first time.

Everything in Děčín started smooth. We practiced hard during the day and partied when we could. The team gave us a shared car, and Rico lived right across from me. His girlfriend, at the time, and now his wife, Julie, came over during the season, and we'd all hang out—trips to Prague, restaurants, or movies. One night, we even drove to Germany since it was only about an hour away, just to switch it up. They had a Burger King there, and we loaded up on food and smashed it on the way home. If there was fun to be had, we were going to find it. Julie also cooked home-cooked meals, sometimes, and invited me over.

The gym had a restaurant attached to it, and the food there was solid. We hit that spot often after practice. I spent hours in the gym every morning, even on game days, getting shots up in the dark, rehearsing the moves I knew I would use later that night. Working gave me peace. Early in the season, everything clicked. I was top five in the league. Dropped 27 and 10 on TV. Had big games against the reigning champions. Everything felt exactly how I had planned and prepared for. Then Christmas break happened, and— and everything shifted.

Rico and I flew home for the holidays. When we left, the team was in fourth place, playing well, and I was performing at a top level. But when we got back... the coach benched me. No warning. No explanation. Just sat me down out of nowhere. It crushed me. I was furious. And if you know me, I'm not a guy who shows a lot of emotion, but I felt tears forming; that's how deep it hit. I went out and played one of my worst games of the season after that. Frustration took over. I stopped working. I partied more. I lost discipline.

Me, Rico, and our other American teammate Kevin were out late—Prague, Děčín, wherever. After games; sometimes, before games. I didn't care. Fans saw us. Management saw us around town. My attitude was, "Forget the coach." But deep down, I knew I was changing in a way that wasn't me. I'd call Lauren and the Davis family, venting about everything. I knew I was better than what I was showing, and I hated that I allowed someone, especially a coach, to break my confidence and push me out of character.

A few games before the end of the regular season, something clicked. I got back in the gym. Started getting my extra shots up. Locked back in. The confidence returned. Even though my role stayed smaller, I was efficient. I even earned Player of the Game in a playoff win at Pardubice—the team Levell had moved to.

Despite the coach changing my role, I still led the team in scoring and rebounding that season. And I had more than enough tape to get myself out and land another deal. I knew for sure I wasn't coming back to the Czech Republic. I loved the people, loved the experiences, but it was time to move on. Me and Rico stayed until all our money was paid. I spent a few more nights painting the town, enjoying the last stretch. Then I flew home to Charlotte, with about $30,000 cash on me. I didn't want to wire it. Looking back, what the hell was I thinking? But I made it through customs and security with no issues somehow.

Once home, I linked back up with Matt and Rusty, who had an apartment in Charlotte. I worked part-time at Barium Springs just to keep something on my résumé, but I didn't need the money; I had plenty. And I spent it recklessly. I went out every weekend. Drinks, food, giving people money, renting cars, buying clothes; the money flew out of my hands as fast as it came in. I wasn't spending much time with Lauren, and our connection was fading. I was living like I was untouchable. Before I knew it, the money was gone. I had never made money like that before, and neither had anyone I knew. I was never taught how to save or invest. In my mind, it wasn't a big deal; I'd make more next season. What I didn't know was that the next season would be the last time I ever played professionally. And it would also be the worst experience of my overseas career—a team that didn't pay me and still owed me money. A hard lesson was waiting for me. And it changed everything.

Poland, Górnik Wałbrzych, was my final stop. One of the strongest leagues. Big names. But terrible management. Missed payments. Cold gyms. A broken thumb most of the year. At first, it seemed like it would be a solid season. The league had teams competing in EuroCup and EuroLeague, so it was supposed to be a real stepping stone. The goal was always the same: play your best games against the top squads so your agent had something real to send out. I averaged about 7 and 5. They promised us a Christmas break, then took it back. Some days, I didn't even leave my apartment.

My teammates were Markus Carr, Chad Barnes, and Ousmane Barro. We were tight. If we weren't practicing, we were together eating, hanging out, or trying to stay sane. I went through two coaches that year. We started the season decent—not many wins, but competitive. But when you drop three, four, five games in a row, somebody's gotta go. The coach who brought me in got fired. That was the beginning of the end. A new coach came in and brought new players with him. Around the same time, rumors started that our sponsors were backing out. If you've ever played overseas, you know what that means: the money is about to stop. The GM tried to calm us down and keep us on the court, but we all knew what was coming.

We kept playing and putting up stats. On off days, we went out, partied, and tried to numb the stress. Then the exits started: Markus left first, then Ous, then Chad. I was the last one standing. It got so bad, I refused to play. Alison and I kept in touch through all of this. She was dealing with the same thing in France during her WNBA offseason. We both decided we weren't going to practices. I remember one day the GM came to my apartment because they always picked us up for practice, and I just didn't come downstairs. A day or two later, they suddenly found the money to pay me. But that didn't last long.

Thankfully, I had saved four or five months of checks and bonuses, so I had a little cushion to take home. But the whole experience left a bad taste in my mouth. Bob, my agent, wasn't much help either. He didn't get his agent fee, so he was frustrated, but at the end of the day, you still want to take care of your players.

I had a few offers to finish the year elsewhere, but between the thumb and the money issues, I was ready to get back to the States. I left with a handful of games remaining once the team confirmed they would stay in the top division. I got a couple thousand they still owed me and a flight home—that was enough for me.

I turned down a few more offers: one back in the Czech Republic, one in Puerto Rico, and another in Mexico for three months. I just wanted to be home. The rest of the money they owed me? Never saw it. Charge it to the game. I didn't know that would be my last season. But the 2008 economic crash destroyed overseas budgets. Offers dropped from eight or nine thousand a month with bonuses down to four or five. I waited. Stayed ready. Turned down bad deals. Finland called. I almost signed. But my heart wasn't in it. That was it. My pro career was over.

Through it all, Europe taught me more than basketball ever could. That discipline matters. That the world is bigger than you think. That money fades. That adapting is a skill. That loneliness makes you tougher. And that no matter where you are… you never fold.

CHAPTER 10

BUILDING BOBW (THE FIRST YEARS)

When I first got home from Poland, Lauren and I were living in Huntersville, and I was trying to figure out what life back in the States was supposed to look like. Everything felt wide open but uncertain. I went back to working at Barium for a while — they always looked out for me whenever I came home. A lot of the kids and families there came from tough backgrounds, and I could relate to that. I understood the weight they were carrying, the chaos they lived in, and how much having a steady adult around could matter. The job gave me structure without trapping me, which was exactly what I needed while I tried to figure out my next steps.

One day, at the Food Lion in Huntersville, I ran into a childhood friend, James Akers. He had gone to Mount Pleasant High School, but we'd known each other for years from hooping around different parks and rec centers. Running into him ended up being exactly what I needed at that moment in my life. After that, me and James started hitting every gym and park in the area. We dominated everywhere we played. Honestly, that stretch might've been some of the best basketball of my life; no pressure, no contracts, just pure hoop. After runs, we'd grab wings at a local bar and watch whatever game was on. Simple routines, but in that season of my life, those moments kept me grounded. me and James stayed close over the years. I was a groomsman in his wedding to Kisha, and he was a groomsman in mine. That's family now. Another bond built through basketball.

When I officially started training kids, it was around 2008–09. I was still working at Barium Springs doing community support work. The schedule was flexible, which let me keep hooping, keep working out, and still keep the door open for overseas opportunities. Most days, I split time between the YMCA in Statesville and the Barium Springs YMCA in Troutman. Being a six-eight Black man in those gyms meant people noticed me immediately. I didn't mind it. I lived in the weight room, played pickup every chance I got, and stayed in the gym putting up shots.

I can't remember the very first parent who asked me to train their child, but I remember the hours. The rhythm. The feeling of pouring into a kid and watching something click. And I definitely remember one of the first players who became like family: **Elizabeth Webb**.

Liz was a sixth grader when I started working with her. She already had so many tools: she could shoot it, handle it, finish at the rim, and she competed every single rep. Her mom, Cindy, and John, treated me like family from the beginning. I'd go to their house in Statesville for dinner; we'd sit around talking, laughing, and just hanging out. I went to Liz's games every chance I got, cheering for her like she was my own. Years later, Bria became close to her too. Liz even stood beside Bria as one of her bridesmaids at our wedding; that's how deep the bond had grown.

I also trained other players early on who helped shape those foundational years of BOBW: Tyra, Tyrin, KP, Garvin, Sarah,

Aavanth, and Evaan. Each one added something different, and each one reminded me why I fell in love with developing players in the first place. To this day, nothing hits quite like running into a former player, or their parents, and hearing how I impacted their lives. Not just as a trainer, not just as a basketball guy, but as a person. Knowing that something I said, taught, or modeled stuck with them… that's the kind of impact that lasts long after the last workout ends.

Another early student was Matt Reyes. From the first day I met him and his family, I knew he was built different. Disciplined, hardworking, locked in. He just had that presence. Basketball was never going to be his end game; his potential was bigger than the court. Sure enough, he graduated from West Point and earned his Expert Infantryman Badge. A lot of the kids we trained over those years ended up doing great things far beyond basketball. That still means more to me than anything.

In the beginning, the business wasn't even called BOBW. It started as Shooting Stars. I knew one thing for sure: I didn't want to name it after myself. I never wanted "Damien Argrett Basketball." I wanted something that felt bigger than me, something other coaches could take ownership in, and a name that represented a mission rather than a person.

Around that time, I met Ron Curry at the Lowe's YMCA in Mooresville. We battled in pickup games constantly and built respect fast. He had just retired from the NFL and was figuring out his next chapter. One morning, we sat at The Daily Grind for breakfast and I pitched the idea of building a basketball-and-football training business together. He was all in.

Those pickup runs at the Y introduced me to some great guys, including Ernest Ruffin, who we called "Ruff," and Pete Philo, who, at the time, was a scout for the Minnesota Timberwolves. Pete even put me through a workout once at the YMCA that had me about ready to pass out. Ruff was an ex-NBA agent who had also represented WNBA players. He even showed up in an episode of *Basketball Wives* back in the day. Both of them became mentors during that early phase—solid guys with real experience, knowledge, and stories that helped shape the direction I was headed. Those connections, conversations, and environment helped lay the groundwork for what would eventually become BOBW, long before the name ever existed.

At that time, Addison, who was from Mooresville, helped Ron get a coaching job at his father's private school coaching football, and Addison also helped us run our very first camp. Ron brought credibility from UNC and the NFL, and once we started building momentum, it all made sense. After running that first camp and looking at other basketball businesses online, the name "Best of Both Worlds" came to me. Part of it was that Jay Z and R. Kelly album. Part of it was how most kids played both football and basketball through high school. Part of it was Ron being national player of the year in both at UNC, and me coming from basketball. If you trained with us, you truly were getting the best of both worlds. Eventually I shortened it to BOBW because it just looked cleaner and stuck easier.

The biggest struggle early on was getting clients, not the one-on-one sessions or small groups, but camps and clinics. The other big struggle was gym space. Before I found Benchwarmers, I was using the Statesville YMCA and Mooresville YMCA. Eventually, people complained about me using the courts for training. I approached both places in hopes of renting space or partnering, but neither had any interest. Someone eventually told me about Benchwarmers. It was mostly a baseball facility with batting cages, a golf simulator, and crossfit space, but they also had a full basketball court that no one was using. That court would change everything.

My first ever clinic had two kids. If that doesn't humble you, nothing will. But if you believe in what you're doing, you don't quit; you pivot. I went around to schools dropping off flyers. Some took them. Some probably tossed them in the trash. Since I was still working full time, BOBW wasn't my only source of income, so I just stayed consistent. The workouts, the small groups, the grind—I kept showing up.

By March of 2011, me and Ron sold out our first official camp together as Shooting Stars. That spring, we officially switched the name to Best of Both Worlds: BOBW.

Ron played a big part in the early days. He ran football workouts, helped with basketball, and brought name recognition and credibility when we needed it. Rick, who owned Benchwarmers, was huge too. He let me use the space for anything basketball related. That summer, we ran our first basketball league. Then we ran a fall league. By the next spring, we were running three leagues: spring, summer, and fall. John started reffing games for us. Tee (Terrence Baxter) jumped in too. The community around us got stronger by the month.

The moment I realized my story wasn't just about me anymore was at the March Madness clinic. The gym was packed with kids eager to learn from me and Ron. Watching them lock in, listen, and trust what we were teaching showed me something deeper; we had more to offer than our ability to play. Our experiences, our lessons, our failures, our wins... all of it meant something to the generation coming behind us. That day, it clicked. My purpose had shifted. Basketball wasn't just something I did anymore; it was something I could pass on. It was the beginning of coaching, teaching, and building what would eventually become BOBW.

The moment I knew BOBW could actually become something real came when the leagues exploded. Nobody in this area was running leagues like that back then. Most rec departments were focused on baseball and softball. Rick had a great relationship with Darrin at Mooresville Parks and Rec, and that connection opened the door for us to use Talbert Rec Center for overflow games once our league outgrew a single court. That partnership was huge; it gave us access to their database, their community, and overnight, our numbers took off. That changed everything.

Ron eventually moved on to a coaching job with the San Francisco 49ers, and from that point on, I ran BOBW on my own until Rico came home and joined me in 2014. Those early years weren't perfect, but they were foundational. We were building something that didn't exist—not here, not in this way. Something the community had never seen before. And even back then, deep down, I knew we were only getting started.

CHAPTER 11

THE GROWTH YEARS
(PRE-COVID)

The years after we officially launched BOBW felt like stepping into something bigger than myself. What started as a couple workouts in the YMCA turned into an operation that was growing month after month, season after season. By 2011, we were ready to take the next step, and that's when the leagues began.

That first summer league at Benchwarmers wasn't anything close to what BOBW would eventually become. We had maybe fifteen teams, one court, and a group of people figuring things out as we went. It was me, Rick, Dan, BJ, CarolAnn, and Big Mike, who would later pass away. I was running around, handling everything: marketing, posting on social media, handing out flyers, and talking to anyone who would listen about the league. Dan and BJ focused on shirts and awards. Mike helped CarolAnn with the database, schedules, and anything computer-related. We didn't have a system; we just had commitment.

Even with all the scrambling, the league had something special from the beginning. It was different. We allowed teams to bring their own full rosters: something no one else in the area was doing. Most leagues wanted everything in-house, but I understood kids had friends, chemistry, and coaches they trusted. Letting people bring their teams made the league more competitive and made families want to be there. That one decision probably grew BOBW faster than anything else in those early years.

Behind the scenes, the partnership between Rick and the Town of Mooresville changed everything for us. Rick had a great relationship with Darrin, who oversaw Parks & Recreation, and the deal they worked out—letting the town's baseball teams use Benchwarmers' batting cages in exchange for us getting court access at Talbert Rec when the league overflowed—was huge. It opened us up to the town's entire database and doubled our numbers almost overnight. A small fifteen-team league slowly grew to three hundred participants, then four fifty, then six and seven hundred during spring and summer seasons. The momentum was real.

The first big moment where I realized BOBW wasn't just an idea anymore was the March Madness Camp we ran at Benchwarmers. It was me, Ron, Addison, and my high school friend, Nestor, helping. We only had two baskets in the whole building, but over fifty kids showed up. It was crowded, loud, chaotic, and perfect. That weekend felt like confirmation: people believed in what we were building, and they trusted us with their kids. You don't forget moments like that.

I was learning business on the fly: how to file an LLC, how to price camps and clinics, how to market correctly, how to communicate, how to organize teams and schedules, how to handle parents, and how to carry myself as someone running something real. There was a lot of trial and error, and plenty of mistakes, but the biggest advantage I had was that I never got comfortable. Each year, we added something new: better marketing, banners, backdrops, awards, rings, videos, photos, social media content, and eventually, our YouTube channel. I didn't want BOBW to look like anything else. I wanted it to feel elite, intentional, and different.

At the same time, my daily life was nothing but a grind. I'd train kids whenever I wasn't working my regular job, host Saturday morning clinics, run camps on school breaks, work late nights preparing league schedules, answer emails, handle payments, and try to be everywhere at once. For a long time, I wanted my hands on everything. I thought that's what leadership looked like. Eventually, I learned you need a real team to grow.

When Rico came home in 2014, he jumped into the AAU side, which I had avoided for years. I didn't want to deal with the drama that came with AAU, but he pushed for it, and I let him take ownership of that part. We started with one team, then met Chuck DiNolfo, who helped us expand. That one team grew into LKN1, then CLT1 later on. The camps and clinics were always profitable; the AAU never really was. People think AAU programs make big money, but unless you're cutting corners, and we weren't, it's not like that. Between gym rentals, coaches' pay, insurance, uniforms, website fees, and admin costs, whatever profit was left usually went right back into branding or events.

AAU brought someone into my life I'm forever grateful for: Shaun Lawrence. I coached his son, Max, and through that, Shaun became one of my closest friends. He often told me I was the best coach Max ever had because I pushed him and helped him believe in himself. Shaun became a brother to me. We golf together, travel together, and he stood beside me as one of my groomsmen at my wedding.

Bria will tell you that he's a big part of me changing for the better. Watching how he treats his wife, Kim, and his kids, how he carries himself as a man, and how he runs his business, Pinnacle Pools, makes me rethink a lot. In my twenties, everything was cars, girls, nightlife, money, and fun. By my thirties, life humbled me and taught me that's not the man I want to be. Having someone like Shaun in my circle helped me level up.

Those years leading up to COVID were fast, tiring, rewarding, and full of growth. BOBW was rising, our leagues were dominating the area, our camps were improving every year, and our name had started traveling far beyond Mooresville. Looking back now, that stretch was the true foundation of everything BOBW has become today.

CHAPTER 12

LOVE, FAMILY, AND BALANCE

I didn't know it at the time, but meeting Bria marked the beginning of a shift in my life I wasn't fully prepared for. Back then, I was still with Lauren, but the truth is simple: I was the problem. I wasn't faithful, I wasn't consistent, and I wasn't showing up like someone ready for a real relationship. Over time, me and Lauren grew apart. She deserved better than what I was giving, and I wasn't in a place to be that for her. Eventually, we went our separate ways. There was no big argument or dramatic ending; just the natural conclusion to something I hadn't handled the right way. It was a chapter I had to learn from, and one that forced me to grow up in ways I didn't realize I needed yet.

After the breakup, I moved into an apartment in Mooresville. It should've been a clean slate, but instead, I was still playing childish games: talking to multiple girls, chasing attention, avoiding commitment, and convincing myself that lifestyle was normal. I wasn't disciplined. I wasn't focused. I wasn't the man I thought I was.

And it was during that time, after Lauren, and moving to Mooresville, that Bria and I started talking seriously.

She was at Belmont Abbey, playing volleyball and living the kind of college life she was supposed to live: structured, competitive, focused, and disciplined. Even at that age, she carried herself with maturity. From early on, she was clear about intentions: if we were going to talk, she wanted it to be just me and only me. But I wasn't ready for that. Not because she wasn't worth committing to—she absolutely was—but because I wasn't ready to give up the lifestyle I was addicted to. I liked her, respected her, felt something real early... but my actions didn't match my feelings.

Our conversations were different: deep, real, and intentional. We talked about family, sports, goals, discipline, confidence, and life. She wasn't playing games. She wasn't out here looking for attention. She knew who she was and what she wanted. We went on little dates; mostly Applebee's happy hour. She was responsible, on time, and focused. Meanwhile, I was still figuring myself out. Eventually, she saw I wasn't ready for the level she expected. And by the time I tried to step up, she didn't trust it. She moved on; and she was right.

We didn't talk for almost three years. During that time, I stayed single. I kept working, building BOBW, growing, and trying to understand who I wanted to become. I thought about her sometimes, but I accepted that I had messed it up. Around then, my cousin, Dashawn, moved in with me. He was grinding: juggling jobs, pushing through school, sleeping on the office couch or in his car when he had to. That era shaped both of us. But before Bria came back into my life, something happened that humbled me in a way nothing else had.

In 2012, I got a DUI. I was out in Charlotte with Nestor and some friends. I didn't feel drunk, but I had a few drinks. I left early, got pulled over for speeding, told the officer the truth, and took the sobriety test because I didn't think I was over the limit. I was wrong. I blew slightly over and was arrested. I spent the night in jail and was released the next morning. The consequences were heavy: court fees, losing my license temporarily, embarrassment, facing the kids who looked up to me, facing my job, and seeing the DUI pop up before anything else when you Googled my name. That moment could've ruined everything. But God knows when to humble you. That DUI forced me to slow down, reflect, and mature.

During that season, I leaned on the people who sharpened me: Dashawn grinding through his own battles, Levell coaching and playing overseas, and Pete and Ruff pushing me to think like a businessman instead of just a trainer. Change wasn't instant. It came from honest reflection, discipline, and accepting that the lifestyle I was living wasn't leading to the future I wanted. I knew I wanted to be a husband one day, and also a father and leader. And I wasn't living like someone who deserved those things.

Then one day, I walked into Outback in Statesville and ran into Bria's best friend, Jackie. She was warm and surprised to see me. I didn't think anything would come from it, but shortly after, Bria reached out. Talking to her again didn't feel like revisiting the past; it felt brand new. Mature. Clean. Like two people meeting at the right time. We went to Dave & Buster's, and the energy was easy, real, and honest. I can't tell you everything we talked about, but I remember the feeling: calm, comfortable, and grown. At the time, Dashawn was still staying with me. Life was chaotic, funny, stressful, and busy, but it was shaping me into the man I needed to be.

By the time Bria came back into my life, I wasn't the same person she met years earlier. I had done the hard work on myself. She didn't have to fix me or carry me; she just added value. She was disciplined, consistent, focused, and driven. Being around her made the next steps in life feel natural. That was the beginning of real balance: love, maturity, responsibility, and purpose, all arriving at the right time. Bria and I started living together in Statesville after I moved into her apartment so we weren't wasting money on two places. We were happy, growing, and taking real steps toward something serious. For us, that meant marriage.

Even with everything we had been through, and even knowing God had brought us back into each other's lives, I was still hesitant. I can't remember the exact argument, but one day, a few months into dating again, Bria and I had a big fight and came close to breaking up. I left the apartment to cool off. When I came back a few hours later, she had gone out and gotten a cat—of all things. I walked in to Bria holding our brand-new kitten, Ron, and all I could do was smile. In that moment, I knew we were going to make this work. It was time for both of us, especially me, to step up.

That same year, I received one of the biggest honors of my life. I was driving to a tournament in Hickory when my phone rang. The name on the screen was one I hadn't seen in a while: Jack Ingram, my professor and friend from Pfeiffer University. We built a strong relationship during my time there; he watched our games, supported our team, and I often helped him run clinics for the local high school girls.

As soon as I saw his name, I had a feeling. It was the call I'd been waiting on for years—the Hall of Fame call. But I didn't let myself believe it until he said the words. Ever since my freshman year, I had dreamed about joining those plaques in the Pfeiffer Hall of Fame. I used to walk past them constantly, studying the names, the stats, and the faces, and trying to imagine how I could earn a place up there one day. After my junior year—second team All-Conference, and our team reaching the NCAA Division II Elite Eight—I knew I had a chance. Becoming an All-American made the possibility even more real. Jack joked with me for a bit before finally saying it: "Damien, congratulations… you're going into the Pfeiffer Hall of Fame."

I was ecstatic. The first call I made was to Bria, then to Rico. Being inducted into a Hall of Fame is something every athlete dreams of. It's not given; it's earned. For me, it validated everything: the work, the sacrifice, the lonely nights, the doubt, and the grind. It was all worth it.

A few months later, in December, I was inducted with Bria and some of my closest family and friends there to support me. Coach John and Dave came. Dave gave an incredible speech about how I arrived at Pfeiffer as a quiet, unsure freshman and grew into one of the best players—and people—he had ever coached. T-Bax was there, along with Rico, Julie, Drew, Dr. King, Lindsey from lacrosse and her husband, Shaun, and even Tony Propst—a guy I looked up to in high school.

I had worked on that speech for months. I wanted it perfect. I read most of it, but I definitely drifted off the page a few times because of the emotion. My guys, Matt, Rusty, and Rick, even came, with Matt flying in all the way from Texas. We've always shown up for each other's big moments, and whenever we're together, it's like no time has passed. I would later be inducted again in 2018 with our 2003–04 team, and there's a good chance our 2004–05 team will get the honor as well.

Bria and Jackie came to the ceremony, and Bria was so proud. She told me later that on the drive up that she and Jackie had talked about how she knew I was the one, and how she could see the real changes I had made. Crazy to think that a year later, I'd be proposing to her. Now, I'm just waiting on the Rowan County Sports Hall of Fame.

That one is tougher to get into, but hopefully, my body of work is enough when the time comes.

Before Kaison was born, even before Bria and I were married, some major relationships in my life had already begun to shift. One of those was with John. He was someone who had played a huge role in my journey, and I'll always appreciate what he did for me, especially during my college years. But adulthood has a way of revealing where relationships stand. He was supposed to go to Vegas with me for my bachelor trip—something planned months in advance. Shaun had taken care of our rooms, so all he needed to do was book his flight. Months passed, and he never did. Eventually, he sent a text saying he wouldn't be going. I didn't argue, but the disappointment sat with me.

Then, a few weeks after I got back from Vegas, he called Bria and told her he wouldn't be marrying us either, even though he had promised he would. That was the moment things shifted for good. I had always shown my appreciation, never letting him pay for anything, and always taking care of him when we were together, but sometimes, distance reveals truth. We drifted apart, and we haven't spoken since. I still speak with his wife from time to time, and I stay connected to his brother, David, on Facebook. I don't hold anger. I'm simply at peace with what our relationship became.

A similar shift happened later with Maurice. We had grown close over the years, but one day, he asked to borrow money. The one time I said I couldn't, he snapped, saying things that weren't true, including that our dad wasn't really my dad. I didn't believe any of it, but hearing it still stung. Not because of the words, but because it showed just how far apart we had grown. That's when I truly learned one of life's hardest lessons: sometimes, you have to let people go. Sometimes you outgrow people. Sometimes a person's season in your life simply ends, no matter how important they once were. And that's okay. You can still love people from a distance. Still pray for them. Still wish them the best. But you don't have to carry every relationship forward into every new chapter of your life.

Around that same time, life started to shift in a different, more positive direction. me and Bria were getting serious, and BOBW was growing fast. Most of the gyms I was using were in Mooresville, so instead of driving back and forth every day, we made the decision to move there. The apartment we found was small but perfect for what we needed: close to everything, affordable, and a place where we could finally build something together. It became our first real home base as a couple; the place where we started laying down roots without even realizing it.

New Year's Eve, 2017, at Shaun and Kim's house was a turning point—the night everything changed. We were all playing Incoherent, laughing, and having fun. Bria pulled a card that read, "WUH HILL EW MARE HEAM HE," and she kept sounding it out, confused. When she finally heard it—"Will you marry me?"—I dropped to one knee. I told her how much she meant to me and how much she had changed my life, and she said yes. The ring didn't fit, even though I tried as best I could to get the size right, but nothing could ruin that moment. Everyone in the room knew exactly what that moment meant.

Our wedding at Rock Barn in 2018 was the best day of my life at that time. Before our first look, I stood with my eyes closed, praying, thanking God for bringing this woman back into my life, and asking Him to bless our marriage. When I finally turned and saw her walking down the cart path… breathtaking. In that moment, every mistake, lesson, and chapter of my life made sense.

That apartment saw everything. Holiday get-togethers with our friends. Game nights full of laughs. Ron sneaking onto the balcony like he owned the place. me and Bria coming home from AAU tournaments and sitting at the kitchen table counting money from BOBW events that Rico and Julie helped us run. It was the place where we grew, struggled, dreamed, planned, and learned each other. The place that showed us what we were capable of as a team.

Leaving it was bittersweet, but the next step was rewarding. We saved, stayed disciplined, and two years later, we bought our first home together—a moment that meant more to me than most people will ever understand. I became the first person in my family to own a home. Doing it with Bria made it even more meaningful. It showed us that together, we could accomplish anything.

After all of that, Bria and I took a quiet beach trip with Kaison. Just the three of us. Life had been chaotic, and getting away felt like a reset we desperately needed. I remember walking down the beach with him, freezing even though the sun was shining bright, then taking him to a park so he could play. In the middle of a world full of noise and uncertainty, having them beside me gave me peace I didn't know I needed. I knew she was the one from the day we locked eyes in that weight room at the YMCA. Funny how life works; how one moment and one glance can change the trajectory of your entire life.

Marriage has shown me that it's not about me anymore; it's about us. Every decision, every move, and every plan, we make together. She makes me better: more intentional, more patient, and more disciplined. And I still remember knowing without a doubt that she was my forever the moment I saw her at Rock Barn, walking toward me with that smile.

She continues to teach me what real love looks like: how to forgive, how to grow with someone, and how to show up the right way. She motivates me to want more for myself, not through pressure, but through the example she sets every day. Bria didn't save me; she met me at the right time. When I finally became the man she always deserved, she believed in me, challenged me, and grew with me. She helps shape the husband, father, and leader I am today.

CHAPTER 13

BUSINESS, BETRAYAL, REBIRTH, PURPOSE

As time went by, BOBW continued to grow. Our relationship with the Town of Mooresville was getting stronger, our travel program kept expanding, and we were always thinking of new ways to take things to another level—especially Rico. We had a great system in place. I handled the BOBW side—camps, clinics, workouts, small groups, emails, social media, and marketing—while Rico focused on the tournaments and building that lane. Even though Rico led the tournament side, I was heavily involved as well. I helped with staffing, made sure we had the startup money for each weekend, handled signage and score sheets, checked that every location had what it needed, ordered food for workers, cleaned gyms afterward—whatever it took to keep things running smoothly.

The operational side came naturally to me. I've always had an eye for detail and the ability to plan ahead for clinics, camps, and creative ideas to grow the business. On the tournament end, Rico ran point with help from Cathy, who had a child on one of our boys' teams. She eventually became his assistant and later helped me once our partnership ended. Cathy kept everything organized—schedules, payments, and communication—and even took over scheduling and emails for our rec teams. Taking those responsibilities off Rico's and Bria's plates allowed him to spend more time networking with coaches and organizations and bringing them into our events.

Anyone who has ever run tournaments knows how much goes into them. Securing gyms, staffing, wristbands, signage, door money, confirming teams, and making sure every spectator pays—it takes months of planning for something that lasts a day or two. We started small with two to four courts, but eventually expanded to events using ten or more. More courts meant more teams and more revenue, but it also meant more expenses and more headaches. We were on the verge of breaking another tournament record when the unexpected hit.

When COVID arrived and the world shut down, it didn't just change the business—it exposed everything. It exposed people's character, priorities, and what really mattered.

A few months later, the day before Kaison was born, we spent time with our friends Kevin and Tennille. Bria sat in their pool, getting some relief from carrying him, while Kevin, Chuck, and I went out on the jet skis. Later, we stopped by Gee and Step's house to eat and talk. The next day, we headed to the hospital in Statesville, not knowing just how much our lives were about to change.

On June 29, 2020, Kaison Elijah Argrett was born. He weighed 9 pounds, 5 ounces, and measured 19.5 inches, already filling the room with a presence bigger than his size. In that moment, everything shifted. Bria and Kaison became the center of my world—the people I cared for most and the reason every decision carried more weight. Basketball, business, and ambition still mattered, but they took a back seat to the joy, responsibility, and love that came with becoming his father. He is, and will always be, our greatest blessing.

Having a baby during COVID was tough, but we didn't go through it alone. Bobbie, Bria's mom, was a constant source of support. She spent many days helping with cooking, cleaning, and simply being there for us when we needed it most.

Alexis and Sandra, who we met through Rico, also became a big part of our lives during that time. Both had played college and professional basketball and worked with us at BOBW for a while. Through that, we became really close. They helped watch Kaison during those early years, and we spent a lot of time together—playing games, cooking out, and just cooling—leaning on each other and finding moments of normalcy during an uncertain season. We even took an unforgettable trip to New Orleans together with Rico, Julie, and a few of Sandra's friends, creating memories that went far beyond basketball and business.

Shaun and Kim were also huge supports for us. They were always willing to lend a hand—watching Kaison, having us over for a meal, or simply being there to listen when things felt heavy. Their presence gave us space to breathe during a season that demanded a lot from us.

Around that same time, church became more important to us as well. We began attending The Cove Church more consistently, and it gave us something steady to lean on. It wasn't about perfection or having everything figured out—it was about grounding ourselves, finding community, and staying connected to something bigger than what we were carrying on our own.

It was during that same stretch that things between me and Rico began to change.

What happened between me and Rico wasn't one single moment; it was a slow drift that eventually turned into a hard split. In the early years, we had built something strong together. Camps, clinics, tournaments, and travel teams—the momentum was real. He was charismatic, well-connected, and could talk to anybody. I was the foundation, the structure, and the builder. Together, it worked... until it didn't.

During COVID, everything tightened—emotions, money, pressure, ego. And somewhere during that stretch, Rico changed. He became more focused on high-profile kids, chasing something bigger in his mind, and distancing himself from the day-to-day grind that built BOBW in the first place. He wanted to be seen, to be the face, to be the guy at the top, even though the business existed long before he ever touched it.

Then came the gym incident—the space we were blessed to use right when everything was reopening. I had promised we would follow every CDC rule, keep numbers low, and keep things controlled. That gym was a lifeline at a time when the whole world felt shut down. Two weeks in, we lost that privilege because Rico misused it. That moment told me everything I needed to know; he was moving for himself, not for us, the kids, or the brand.

Not long after, he got access to a gym in Mountain Island, about fifty minutes away on a good day from Mooresville. The rent was a couple thousand dollars a month, and he thought it would be a great idea for us to take it on since most gyms were still closed. To me, it didn't make sense. Most of our players and families were in Iredell County. I didn't see them driving all the way to Charlotte for basketball, and I didn't believe we'd make enough money doing training out of a space that far from our clients. Rico didn't want to hear that. He was convinced it would work, and he rented the space without me.

The last real conversation we had was the one that broke everything. He told me he was focused on "bigger things" and needed me to step up with tournaments, as if I hadn't built this business from scratch, or I somehow wasn't holding my weight. After the years of work, foundation, relationships, and sacrifice, he made it sound like I was the one falling short. That was the moment I realized our partnership was done.

Bria had been frustrated with him for a long time too. She saw the same changes I saw: the ego, inconsistency, and lack of respect. She protected me even when I didn't fully see what was happening. COVID didn't create the problems; it just removed the distractions and showed who people really were.

When I walked away from CLT1, it wasn't emotional. It was necessary. The separation wasn't messy or loud; it was quiet, final, and clear. I rebranded. BOBW was always mine, so I took my name, my work, my vision, and my future with me. I changed the paperwork, designed a new logo, rebuilt the travel program into BOBW Elite and later Lady BOBW Elite, and got back to doing what built the brand in the first place: serving kids, growing players, and building something that would last.

The part that hurt wasn't the business ending; it was the trust breaking. The isolation that followed was real. I didn't know who was truly with me or who would leave next. I guarded my circle. I protected my coaches. I watched everything closely because I wasn't going to let anyone jeopardize what I built ever again. But that's when I realized something important: the right people don't leave. Evan stayed. Steven stayed. David stayed. Cathy stayed. They didn't choose clout or convenience; they chose loyalty. That showed me who my real team was.

And in that same season, when everything felt uncertain, something else was growing: my family, my purpose, and my clarity. After COVID, me and Bria sold our first home—the home we thought would be our forever home, and which we brought Kaison to when he was born. We made a six-figure profit off that sale, which we never imagined when we bought it. That win opened doors for us: investing in rental properties, building spec homes, and taking our financial life to another level. It showed us that even in chaos, blessings still come.

We took a beach trip that year; just me, Bria, and Kaison. And it was exactly what we needed. Life had been chaotic for months, nonstop noise, nonstop stress, and somehow, the three of us stepping away brought everything back into focus. I remember standing on the beach with Kaison, freezing cold even though the sun was shining bright. We walked up and down the shoreline, just talking and laughing, then took him to a park so he could play. In a world full of uncertainty, having them right there beside me brought a peace I hadn't felt in a long time. It reminded me what really mattered and who I wanted to build my life with.

The biggest breakthrough for BOBW came around that same period, after the split. That's when everything truly took off. The league grew faster than I ever imagined: packed clinics, sold-out camps, thriving travel teams, and a level of consistency that families could feel. Before long, we became the largest independent youth basketball program in the entire Mooresville and Lake Norman area. And it wasn't because we were trying to be the biggest; it happened because we committed to being the best. The structure, the experience, the development, the culture—nobody matched it. We built something intentional, something parents trusted, and something kids loved to be part of. It became a turning point not just for the program, but for me as a man, a coach, and a leader.

After COVID, life slowed down for everybody. It gave me time to think about purpose, impact, and what I wanted to build long-term. That's when Jimmie, the principal at Woodland Heights, reached out. We had known each other for years from playing pickup, and over time, that turned into a genuine friendship. When he asked me to step in and help the boys' basketball program, it felt natural. I didn't come in with a grand plan, I came in to guide kids, teach them, and be the steady voice I needed at their age.

Coaching at Woodland Heights became something special. We won back-to-back championships in 2023 and 2024, but the wins weren't the biggest part of it. Watching those kids grow, as players, as teammates, and as young men, was the real reward. Some of them are now being recruited in different sports at the high school level. I don't claim to be the reason, but I hope the example I set helped them believe in what they were capable of.

Before the split between me and Rico, Chris Carr had already come on board with our BOBW Elite travel teams. His sons played in our programs, and he brought a wealth of experience, knowledge, and professionalism to everything he touched. When the split happened, he made the decision to stay with me and continue building with BOBW, which something I will always respect and appreciate.

Chris became an important part of not just Woodland Heights, but BOBW as a whole. He's one of the sharpest basketball minds I've worked with; he sees the game in a way that elevates everyone around him. More than that, he became someone I trust—a steady voice, a dependable presence, and a genuine friend. His commitment to our kids and to our mission helped strengthen everything we were building.

Around that same time, all the community work we had been doing through BOBW—feeding families, giveaways, workshops, and supporting kids—started feeling bigger than the moment. We'd been doing the work from the heart for years, but after COVID, I made it official and turned BOBW Cares into a 501(c)(3). Not for recognition, but for structure, accountability, and the chance to build something that would last long after me. And through that process, certain people played major roles, each in their own way.

Antonio had always been solid. A business owner, respected by everyone, and someone who supported every program we ran: giveaways, workshops, and our middle school all-star game. My bond with him was built on trust, consistency, and years of showing up for the community together. Rakeem was cut from that same cloth. Dependable, humble, and always willing to help without needing credit. He supported everything, from meal services, to events, to the all-star game. My relationship with him grew through years of working side-by-side serving families and kids.

Geo stepped in wherever he was needed. Helping get kids to workshops, supporting families directly, assisting at programs; he played a major role in connecting us to kids who might have been overlooked. My connection with him grew through service and a shared belief in giving back. David became my right hand with BOBW Cares. His passion for helping people matches mine. From leading workshops, to serving meals, to handling behind-the-scenes work, he's been consistent every step of the way. My bond with him grew through countless hours of service, leadership, and purpose-driven work.

Evan was there through the travel seasons and even at Nationals that summer in Myrtle Beach. He eventually moved back home to Detroit, but my bond with him was built through long days in the gym, long weekends on the road, and a shared commitment to helping kids. When Evan moved, Steven stepped up and took on more of the travel responsibilities. Dependable, steady, and always willing to do whatever was needed. My connection with him grew through consistency and the dedication we shared for helping the kids we serve. Each relationship was different. Each one mattered in its own way. It wasn't one big bond; it was individual bonds built through trust, work, and shared purpose.

Coaching and community work became the balance I never knew I needed. One sharpened my leadership. The other taught me humility and service. Together, they shaped the man I am today. And the moment I knew I was exactly where I was supposed to be came one summer at Nationals in Myrtle Beach. Our teams had just finished competing, and I was standing there with Bria and Kaison, with Steven, David, Evan, and Geo nearby; all of us wrapping up another long season. I looked around and felt something I hadn't felt in a long time: peace. Not excitement. Not hype. Just peace. A calm that only comes when you've made the right decisions, even when they were hard. I realized I had built something real. Something strong. Something mine. And I wasn't doing it alone; I was doing it with the right people beside me.

This chapter of my life taught me everything: People can change. Loyalty matters. Integrity matters even more. You don't lose real blessings; you lose distractions. And sometimes, God removes people because you were praying for growth. Walking away from Rico wasn't losing a business partner. It was shedding a weight that kept me from becoming the man, the husband, the father, and the leader I was supposed to be.

As BOBW grew, so did I. And the more I leaned into my purpose, the clearer everything became: life, fatherhood, business, faith, and the legacy I want to leave. This is what I want to leave you with: Life will hit you with things you don't deserve. People will disappoint you. Doors will close. Plans will fall apart. But you can't fold. You don't stop. You keep stepping. You keep believing. You stay solid even when others aren't. Treat people right. Love the ones who love you. Protect your name. Protect your peace. And never let ego, bitterness, or fear make decisions for you. Your journey is yours. Run it with integrity. Run it with purpose. Run it with love. Run it with faith. Because when you show up as the real you—consistently, humbly, and honestly—everything meant for you will find its way to you.

This chapter is the end of the struggle... but the beginning of the man I became. My whole life, I felt like I was racing something: time, mistakes, expectations, and even my own past. But the truth is, the clock was never my enemy. It was my teacher. Every setback was a reset. Every loss shaped my hunger. Every challenge taught me who I was and who I refused to be. And now, I'm not running from anything. I'm running toward everything God has for me: my family, my purpose, and the thousands of kids whose lives cross paths with mine through BOBW. The clock doesn't control me anymore. I set the pace. I set the standard. And I'm exactly where I'm meant to be.

Letter To The Reader

If you've made it to these final pages, thank you. Thank you for walking with me through the gyms, the long nights overseas, the heartbreaks, the victories, the mistakes, the growth, and the blessings that shaped who I am today. My hope is simple: that my story gives you something you can hold on to. Not because I'm perfect—I'm far from it—but because life has a way of showing all of us that the clock is always ticking. And still, every day, you get a choice: keep going or give up. Stand tall or fold. Grow or stay the same.

I pray this book helps you choose growth. I pray it reminds you that your past doesn't disqualify you, your failures don't define you, and your story isn't finished unless you quit. Whatever you're facing or whatever season you're in, keep your faith strong, keep your circle tight, keep your work honest, and keep your purpose first. And when you feel the pressure, and life hits you the hardest... Remember who you are.

Remember what you've survived. Remember what's waiting on the other side if you don't quit. Thank you for reading my story—for letting me share my heart, my journey, my lessons, and my truth.

Against the clock, always,

Damien

Thank You

To everyone who has been a part of my journey, thank you.

To my mother, Joanne, whose love, strength, and sacrifice shaped the foundation of who I am.

To my father, Morris Holmes, your passing lit a fire in me that has never gone out. I carry you with me in everything I do.

To my sister, Tanya, solid since day one, always keeping me grounded and supported.

To Coach John Davis, who believed in me early, pushed me, and guided me both on and off the court.

To Coach Dave Davis, who demanded excellence and taught me how to carry myself like a man.

To Kim Davis, for loving me like your own son and being a constant source of warmth throughout my journey.

To Mrs. Gore, may you rest in peace. Thank you for seeing something in me long before I ever saw it in myself.

To Bria and Kaison, my purpose, my strength, and my why. Everything I continue to build is for you.

And to every kid, parent, teammate, friend, mentor, coach, and supporter who has crossed my path, thank you for trusting me, believing in me, and allowing me to be a part of your story. You all helped shape the man and the mission behind this book.

This book exists because of all of you.

All the best,
Damien

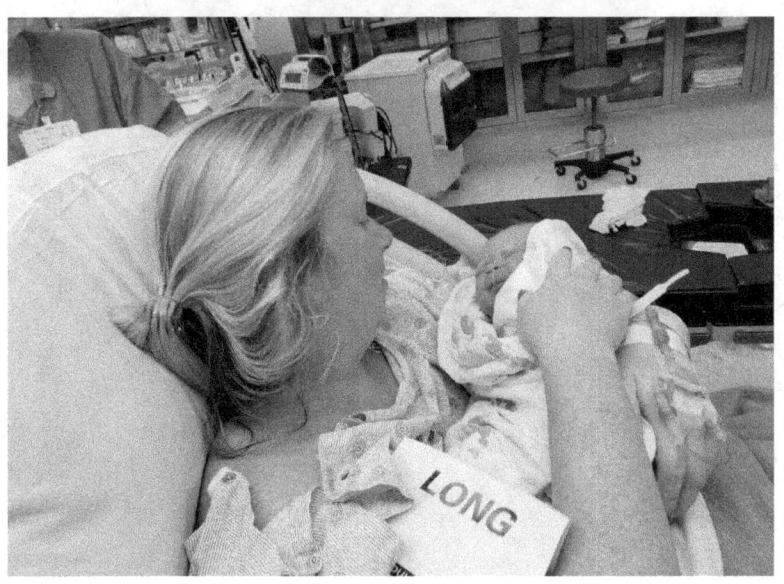

135

NCAA DIVISION II ALL-AMERICAN CANDIDATE

6'8" - Senior
Forward
Kannapolis, NC

Pfeiffer University
FALCONS

DAMIEN ARGRETT

20.1 PPG, 5.8 RPG
IN 20.19 MINUTES OF PLAYING TIME (THRU 2-14-05)

2004-2005 INDIVIDUAL Highlights:
- Statistics projected over 40 minute game: 35.9 ppg 9.77 rpg
- 1st in CVAC in Scoring
- 1st in CVAC in Shooting Percentage
- 20.1 PPG, 5.8 RPG
- 35 Points in 21 Minutes vs. Limestone
- 27 Points in 25 Minutes vs. Mt. Olive
- 26 Points, 9 Rebounds in 18 Minutes vs. Queens
- 24 Points in 18 Minutes vs. Lees McRae
- 24 Points in 23 Minutes vs. Coker
- 21 Points vs. Gannon
- Has Scored More Points Than Minutes Played 7 Times

2004-2005 TEAM Highlights:
- 18-3 through 2-13-05
- Nationally ranked (as high as #7)
- #1 in East Region
- 1st in Team Scoring in Country
- 2-0 vs. #2 Ranked Mt. Olive

Career Highlights:
- 1000 Point Scorer
- 2003-2004 CVAC
- 62% Career FG %

AWARDS:
- CVAC Player of the Week - 1-24-05

"Damien is the most improved player in our league (CVAC). His stats are particularly impressive when you realize he only plays half the game as we play 10-12 guys per game"

- Dave Davis
Pfeiffer Head Basketball Coach

Jan. 30, 1998

On their way

...M. South Rowan's chorus rehearses with director Jan Gore, right, as they prepare

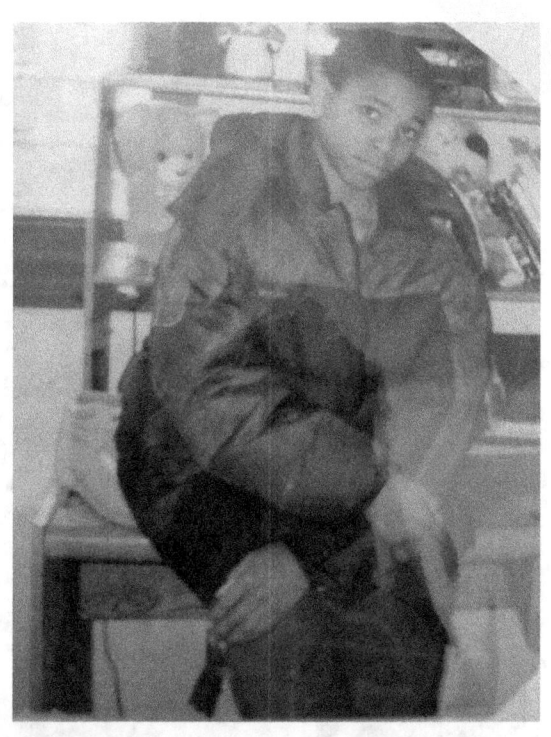